The EUROPEAN ROOTS of
CANADIAN
IDENTITY

The European Roots of Canadian Identity

PHILIP RESNICK

broadview press

Library and Archives Canada Cataloguing in Publication

Resnick, Philip, 1944-
The European roots of Canadian identity / Philip Resnick.

Includes bibliographical references and index.
ISBN 1-55111-705-3

1. Canada—Civilization—European influences.
2. National characteristics, Canadian.
I. Title.

FC97.R478 2005   971   C2005-901160-2

Broadview Press, Ltd. is an independent, international publishing house, incorporated in 1985. Broadview believes in shared ownership, both with its employees and with the general public; since the year 2000 Broadview shares have traded publicly on the Toronto Venture Exchange under the symbol BDP.

We welcome comments and suggestions regarding any aspect of our publications—please feel free to contact us at the addresses below or at broadview@broadviewpress.com / www.broadviewpress.com

North America
Post Office Box 1243,
Peterborough, Ontario, Canada K9J 7H5
TEL (705) 743-8990; FAX (705) 743-8353

3576 California Road,
Orchard Park, New York, USA 14127

E-MAIL customerservice@broadviewpress.com

UK, Ireland and Continental Europe
NBN Plymbridge.
Estover Road, Plymouth PL6 7PY, UK
TEL 44(0) 1752 202301
FAX 44 (0) 1752 202331
FAX ORDER LINE 44 (0) 1752 202333
CUST. SERVICE cservs@nbnplymbridge.com
ORDERS orders@nbnplymbridge.com

Australia & New Zealand
UNIREPS University of New South Wales
Sydney, NSW 2052
TEL 61 2 9664099; FAX 61 2 9664520
E-MAIL infopress@unsw.edu.au

Broadview Press gratefully acknowledges the financial support of the Government of Canada through the Book Publishing Industry Development Program for our publishing activities.

Cover design by Mike Young, Black Eye Design
Typeset by Liz Broes, Black Eye Design

Printed in Canada

CONTENTS

PREFACE

I came to Firenze to forget Peru and the Peruvians for a while,
and suddenly my unfortunate country forced itself upon me
this morning in a most unexpected way.

Mario Vargas-Llosa, *The Storyteller*

Sometimes, it is when you are thousands of kilometres away from
home that you begin to see things in a new light. That proved to be
my case during the academic year 2002–03, when I found myself in
Paris, where I took up a one-year appointment to the Chair in
Canadian Studies at the University of Paris III–Sorbonne Nouvelle.
The opportunity to spend an academic year in Paris (a city where I
had lived for a number of years as a student in an earlier incarna-
tion) was, of course, attractive for all sorts of reasons. Cultural, to be
sure—expositions, museums, films, plays. Intellectual—the wide
range of seminars, colloquia, and discussion forums; the bookstores
with their stream of new publications; great holding libraries like
the Bibliothèque Nationale de France at its new location in the
thirteenth arrondissement overlooking the Seine. Aesthetic—the
beauty of the city's buildings and Haussmannian avenues; the
planned symmetry of the Luxemburg Gardens around the corner
from where we lived; the cupolas of the Sorbonne, the Senate, the
Institut du Monde Anglophone. The presence of history—monu-
ments, memorials, and, especially, plaques. Plaques commemorate
Olympe de Gouges (she of *The Declaration of the Rights of Woman
and the Citizen* of 1791) and the proscribed Condorcet (he of the
Essay on the Future of the Human Condition of 1794) both on the
cobble-stoned rue de Servandoni fending its way from the rue de
Vaugirard down to the Église St. Sulpice. Plaques honour Joseph

7

Roth, the great Austrian novelist and chronicler (along with Robert Musil) of the collapse of the Austro-Hungarian Empire, and Camille Claudel, Rodin's muse and surrogate, slipping into the madness of her final decades at the Quai d'Anjou on the Île St-Louis. Another at the former Hotel York on the rue Jacob commemorates where the Treaty of Paris of 1783 establishing the United States of America was signed.

But there was something more to the year that made it resonate for me in an unanticipated way. I am referring to the Iraqi crisis, spinning out for months at the United Nations with the debate about whether weapons of mass destruction in Iraq (none were subsequently to be found) could in fact be destroyed short of war; to the streets of the world's capitals and cities, where millions marched on February 15, 2003 to shout their opposition to the impending juggernaut; to the decision of the Bush Administration, with its loyal British and Australian allies in tow, to begin hostilities on March 19, 2003; and to the occupation of the country and the regime change that followed. Because France, with Jacques Chirac freshly re-elected as President in May 2002 and the ebullient Dominique de Villepin as his foreign minister, played a leading part in trying to stymie the American war machine, my being on the European side of the Atlantic was a lot more invigorating than might have been the case at some other time. Because Canada, not known for saying "No" to the United States on major issues of foreign or defence policy, actually had the temerity to side with the French, the Germans, the Russians, the Latin Americans, the Africans, indeed most of the countries of the world in its opposition to a unilateral American-initiated attack on Iraq, I was all the happier to be a Canadian.

And it got me thinking. How was it that Canadians, no less North American in their geography, their lived habitat, their economic structures than their American neighbours to the south, were, in a number of other ways, a very different kind of North American? Was it simply a question of United Empire Loyalists on the English Canadian side and "Je me souviens" on the French Canadian—the stuff of history books and political debates of an earlier era? Or could there be something else at work, even at the beginning of the twenty-first century, something that in some mysterious fashion makes present-day Canadians—in all their linguistic and cultural diversity—rather different political and social animals from Americans?

But wherein lay the differences? The Canadian identity question has been flogged so often, that, at first, I shuddered to even address it. But the months passed, and autumn in Paris turned to winter with its rains and leaden skies so reminiscent of Vancouver, winter turned to spring with its greenery and open-air terrasses, and finally spring gave way to summer with its short-sleeve weather. And the question continued to haunt me.

Somewhere in the course of the year, I began to grope my way towards an answer to this question. And that answer now takes the form of the essay that follows, a reflection, all said and done, on the European roots of Canadian identity and on the subtle ways in which these continue to mark our own quite distinct development as a country in the northern part of North America.

Three acknowledgements. The first is to Jessica Delaney, a UBC MA student in European Studies, for research assistance with bibliographical sources during the academic year 2003–04. The second is to Karen Taylor for her professional copy-editing of the manuscript for Broadview Press. The third is to my wife Mahie, Canadian and European, who has provided no small amount of the inspiration for this essay.

PR
Paris and Vancouver

CHAPTER ONE

THE CANADIAN ENIGMA

What I take to be the Canadian enigma is caught up with a specifically Canadian set of challenges. These challenges stem from Canada's ongoing history as a North American society, with a predominantly British and French cast to its original population, living cheek by jowl with the most powerful country of the modern world and absorbing, over time, a bewildering mixture of people of diverse ethnic backgrounds into its population.

The Canadian enigma is further caught up with what, at the level of the imagination, one might call a contested form of national identity. By this I mean a persistent sense of doubt about whether Canada—a thinly populated, continent-sized triumph of history over geography—will endure; about its relationship to its powerful North American neighbour; about whether Canadians have a distinct set of values that help to define exactly who they are.

Canada, in certain respects, is an odd kind of nation-state. It has been in existence as a federation ever since the creation of the Dominion of Canada in 1867; as a sovereign state at least since the Statute of Westminster of 1931; as a constitutionally modern country since Pierre Trudeau's 1981–82 patriation of the BNA Act with the addition of a Charter of Rights and Freedoms and an amending formula. Yet few other countries, certainly with the level of economic and social development that Canada has achieved, seem to be as addicted to what one might call the identity game, to a version of "To be or not to be?"

Twice in the past twenty-five years, at the time of the 1980 and 1995 referenda in Quebec on sovereignty, Canada found itself faced with the distinct possibility of political break-up. In 1988, at the time of the free trade debate and election, many wondered whether closer continental integration with the United States might not spell the end of Canada as a fully independent state. Canada was to survive both crises, but not without damage to the collective psyche.

It is an open secret that the French Canadian/Quebec sense of identity is not the same as that of English-speaking Canadians. This difference was already evident at the time of the Confederation Debates of the 1860s, during the Riel controversy of the 1880s, and during the conscription crises of both world wars. What was new about the events of 1980 and 1995 was that they brought home to a majority of Canadians outside Quebec that there was a palpable possibility that a majority of Quebecers might actually prefer to hive off on their own, leaving it for the rest of Canada to reconfigure itself as a fragmented union from sea to sea with a large foreign chunk in its midst. Not an entirely happy prospect for Canadians, for whom the whole of the northern part of North America constitutes the geographical boundaries of their imagined community.

If the danger of Quebec separation has receded for the moment—the Liberal victory in the 2003 Quebec election brought that home—there remains a lingering doubt among Canadians as to whether the bonding of Quebecers with Canada will ever be more than a significantly thinner version of their own, viz. the Bloc Québécois' stellar performance in the 2004 federal election. In other words, the Canadian predicament remains one of divided loyalties, especially where Quebec and the rest of Canada is concerned, something that makes impossible the complete unity that so many on the English Canadian side would like to realize.

NAFTA, for its part, has reinforced north-south economic ties in a country where the east-west connection is an often fragile thing. It has led many Canadians to wonder whether, faced with insatiable demands from business elites and sections of the corporate-controlled mass media to align ourselves on the American market model, we can sustain the type of social programs or cultural policies that have characterized Canada over the past fifty years. These fears have been further strengthened in the aftermath of the Al-Qaeda attacks on the World Trade Centre and the Pentagon of September 11, 2001 by strong pressures coming from the United States, for Canadian integration with the new security doctrine of the Bush administration.

These are the more visible parts of the Canadian identity conundrum to which I will return later in this essay. But I would like to probe a little more deeply into the underlying self-doubt that characterizes Canadians. For if it is historically grounded, as I strongly suspect, it requires a rather different type of perspective from one simply born of recent events.

On the French Canadian side, the British Conquest of 1759 ended the dream of a French empire in North America once and for all. It also ended all hopes for the significant extension of the French-dominated heartland of New France into other parts of North America, inducing in its place a type of siege mentality, in which survival became the dominant ideology. That an increasingly clerically dominated Quebec would have conflictual relations with a post-revolutionary France that spurned the role of eldest daughter of the Church only reinforced a sense of political isolation. The conflict turned the more reform-minded elements in French Canadian society into pariahs, fostering a clerically tinged, inward-looking nationalism, at odds with emerging, industrial values. Quebec, in a number of important respects down to the 1960s, was in North America but not of it. Clerical domination helped give an old regime cast to Quebec's political system, of which the Gouin, Taschereau and Duplessis governments, with their paternalistic practices, were perfect illustrations.

So far so good, where a now familiar reading of the French Canadian experience is concerned. But what if something else were also involved, a persistent refusal to let go of structures of authority that had been inherited from an earlier period and that marked French Canadian society in a way that would never entirely disappear? Could it be that French Canadians were not only French-speaking North Americans, but also quite consciously un-American in their mentality, as their failure to go along with the thirteen colonies at the time of their revolution or their failure to follow the path of liberal revolution in 1837–38 would suggest? Could they, in their own idiosyncratic way, have been adhering to pre-modern European structures of being, even while carving out an existence for themselves as a community in the new world?

If we cast a side-glance at a number of other Catholic peoples in the old world, we may begin to get a feel for what was at stake: the

Basques, for example, with their infatuation for the Carlist cause in the nineteenth century, for ethnic and linguistic purity and for their medievally derived Fueros; the Irish refusing to be absorbed into a United Kingdom, ascendant imperial power that it may have been; or the Poles, the Christ among the nations, sticking tenaciously to their cultural and religious values in the face of the geopolitical catastrophe visited upon them by the three Partitions. This refusal of the modern—in the French Canadian case, of the Protestant, commercial version of the modern so closely associated with the English/American way—was a strategy that made sense at the community level. It came with a high price tag, where control over the commanding heights of the economy, the quality of education, especially technical and scientific education, and the freedom of opinion and debate within French Canadian society were concerned. But it allowed that society to survive in what many felt to be an alien, hostile climate, and, in doing so, eventually to modernize its institutions at a later day—but on its own terms. In other words, *la survivance* was a strategy for continuing to lead a more European-type existence, permeated by old-fashioned ideas about religion, the agricultural vocation, organic identity, and constituted authority, on a continent where the emerging hegemon, the United States, had consciously turned its back on Europe and all its works.

On the English Canadian side, the refusal of the American Revolution was less anachronistic than among the French Canadians. The Loyalists who migrated north of the border were kith and kin to those who stayed behind to establish the United States. They were mostly Protestant, and no less given to commercial-type activity than their thirteen colony counterparts. But if they wanted to remain British, it was in good part out of loyalty to an imperial mission that had made Britain (more than Portugal, Spain, the Netherlands, or France) the leading force of European expansion overseas. Britain, in its way, was also Europe, albeit with its own very particular combination of ordered liberty and ancient institutions. Herein was to lie the political inspiration for her colonial offshoots overseas.

What is striking about the British North American mind frame was a sense of the supremacy of British values. The same relentless energy that newly minted Americans were to pour into lauding the

14

virtues of their new nation was, on the Canadian side of the border, to go into extolling the virtue of things British. Whether it came to the mixed character of the British constitution, to the role of a hereditary monarchy, or, most importantly, to the role of British parliamentary or legal institutions, the mother country, for most colonial politicians, was the source of all good. While disdaining the democratic and republican excesses of American (or French) institutions, Canadians were to champion the more balanced, evolutionary character of British ones, which had made its empire the greatest one known to modern times.

To be a Canadian, at least until 1947, the year of the Canadian Citizenship Act, was to be a British subject in more than name. It was, on the English Canadian side, to imply a solidarity with empire that on three occasions (1899, 1914, and 1939) was to see Canadians engaged in war at Britain's side. And the two most important of those wars saw Canadian troops in the European theatre, bringing home through Ypres and Vimy Ridge and later through Dieppe, Normandy, and the liberation of Holland just how much of a European actor, albeit an extra-European power, Canada really was.

That same European involvement was to be the source of extreme tension where Canadian unity was concerned, given the visceral opposition in French Canada to compulsory engagement in overseas wars in support of the British imperial cause, and this despite the involvement of France at the side of Britain in both world wars. The major source of identity on the English-speaking side until 1945, namely the British connection, a family connection for so many, was fundamentally rejected on the French Canadian one. Hence arose one of the paradoxes of Canadian national identity: the more intense the desire for British external connections on the English Canadian side, the stronger the resistance from Quebec.

Yet as a greater Canadian nationalism was to emerge in English Canada from the 1920s on, and to develop more powerfully still in the decades following World War II, that new nationalism was to come face to face with a competing nationalism in Quebec. This competition was less evident at first, as judicial appeals to the Privy Council were abolished in 1949, as Canadian-born governors-general took the place of British appointees, or as the term "Dominion" was gradually phased out of use by the federal government. But by the 1960s, conscious attempts at fostering Canadian identity (e.g., through the maple leaf flag or through Expo 1967) fell afoul of a competing tendency to foster a new Quebec identity in the aftermath of the Quiet Revolution. Hence a second paradox of Canadian national identity: the more intense its articulation on the English Canadian side, the greater the counter-resistance it evokes in Quebec.

Nor was this the end of the story. In the aftermath of the Royal Commission on Bilingualism and Biculturalism, Canada was to adopt not only a policy of two official languages, but also one of multiculturalism. At one level, multiculturalism was simply long overdue recognition of the role that so-called third force Canadians had played in the peopling and building of Canada. At another, it was implicit acknowledgement of a degree of cultural diversity that was to become even more apparent as successive censuses showed the percentage of Canada's population of neither British nor French origin approaching 40 per cent and the visible minority component of Canada's population increasing dramatically in the aftermath of a new non-discriminatory Immigration Act in 1967.

There is, however, a paradox in using multiculturalism to frame Canadian identity, as was to become common practice in the aftermath of the adoption of the Charter of Rights and Freedoms and of the Multiculturalism Act of 1988. By insisting on the role of governments in furthering the multicultural character of Canada, there was an implicit danger of undercutting elements of shared citizenship in a country with a weaker sense of national identity than that to be found in most western states. Conversely, the pursuit of cultural diversity was a potentially innovative way of addressing the question of who constituted the national "we group" in a country marked by stark divisions between the two founding groups, English and French. We will need to examine a little later in this essay whether official multiculturalism has made it easier or more difficult to come to terms with core elements of Canadian identity.

The aboriginal component of Canadian identity became a more salient feature in political discussions of the 1980s and 1990s. Sections 25 and 35 of the Charter gave a new prominence to aboriginal treaty rights, and subsequent rulings by the courts, especially the Supreme Court of Canada, were to reinforce this prominence.

True, the sweeping suggestions for nation-to-nation relations contained in the Royal Commission Report on Aboriginal Peoples were not to be adopted in any wholesale fashion. And progress on aboriginal land claims, while significant in northern Canada, has been positively sluggish in a province like British Columbia. Nonetheless, at the symbolic level today there is a sense that Canada is made up of three founding peoples, not two. This inclusion of aboriginal peoples in the national "we group" can be seen as long overdue recognition of the historical origins of the country, though it also poses challenges to the way in which we conceive of Canadian identity.

This brings me to the most formidable challenge to Canadian identity—namely, Canada's close proximity to the United States. It may seem odd to place so much weight on the mere chance of geography that has placed Canada on the same North American continent as our neighbour to the south. After all, countries like Poland or the Czech Republic share close proximity with Germany or Russia, yet there is little doubt that they are very different European countries for all that. The same can be said about Thailand, Malaysia, or Vietnam with respect to China or India. Why, then, should the American connection so preoccupy Canadians and lead them to question what makes them who they are?

The answer lies in part in the formidable economic and strategic ties that bind Canada to the United States and in the radically unequal power relations between the two countries. For despite notable differences in political culture, to which I will return in due course, there is a tendency to harp on the similarities. Not only do most Canadians share the same language with Americans, but also both are very closely integrated at the economic level, have a similar fascination with technological innovation, and inhabit the same immense geographical spaces so lacking in much of Europe.

There is also a sense of constituting new societies when compared to European ones with their much older histories. The founding of Quebec or of Massachusetts only goes back four centuries, a relative moment when compared to the much greater antiquity of Mediterranean societies. While West and Central European societies (e.g., France, Germany, Holland, England, or

Poland) also have many more centuries of continuous history underpinning them than do either the United States or Canada. Canada is of the New World, not the Old. And this is reinforced by a constant coming and going across a border that, until September 11, 2001, was permeable to the highest degree. Millions of Americans are of Canadian origin and hundreds of thousands of Canadians of American origin; "Children of a common mother," reads the sign on the Peace Arch between British Columbia and the State of Washington. The present and the future loom larger, in the minds of many on both sides of the border, than the distant past. Similar sagas, such as continental expansion, railway construction, and the settling of the West, characterize both countries' histories.

But Canada, as the less populated, economically and strategically weaker of the two countries, has always had the complexes associated with a dependent position. Not that Canadian dependency vis-à-vis the United States has ever been as extreme as that of the smaller Latin American countries, for example, or that of various American client states of the post-World War II period in Asia, Africa, or the Middle East. Still, the Canadian disposition, going back to the time of Confederation, was to see the United States as an older Brother Jonathan. The United States was sometimes to be feared—as at the time of the Fenian Raids in the late 1860s or when the Speaker of the American House of Representatives in 1910 dreamed of the Stars and Stripes flying from the North Pole to Central America. At other times it was to be embraced—as during the critical moments of World War II when Great Britain faced Nazi Germany by itself, and Canada's own security seemed under threat, or during the Cold War era, when Canadian public opinion, by and large, saw in the Soviet Union a threat to Canadian and western interests.

The fact remains that the United States has never left Canadians indifferent, casting its shadow over its neighbour to the north long before it was to become the great power that it is today. Some of the most tumultuous moments in Canadian electoral history (1891, 1911, 1988) have revolved around our relations with the United States. And the Canadian identity question, for many, can be reduced to a simple and straightforward question: "What, if anything, makes Canadians different from Americans?"

My answer, if I may tip my hand in this introductory chapter, goes as follows: "*What differentiates Canadians from Americans is the fact that Canadians remain a good deal more European in their sensibilities and will continue to be the more European part of North America into the foreseeable future.*" This is what the rest of this essay will seek to map out.

CHAPTER TWO

PARTICULARISTIC VS. UNIVERSALISTIC IDENTITIES

It is a well-known feature of Canadian history that this country, unlike the United States, was not born of revolution. Instead of the *novus ordo seculorum* (the new order of the ages) that the American founding fathers set out to create after the success of the thirteen colonies in the revolutionary wars, Canada's founding fathers were satisfied with achieving Dominion status within the British Empire, with a constitution modelled on that of Great Britain. French Canadians, for their part, the failed rebellions of 1837–38 aside, had imbibed little of the revolutionary spirit from either France or the United States, and were to pursue a decidedly counter-revolutionary course with a strong dose of traditional Catholic doctrine to guide them. If France had betrayed its mission as eldest daughter of the Church in the aftermath of 1789, Quebec, down until the Quiet Revolution of the early 1960s, would not.

The exact consequences of this non-revolutionary trajectory have been the subject of much commentary. Some have read into this path a more conservative disposition on the Canadian side, as compared to the American. "The subject matter in Canadian schools suggested a respect for inherited traditions.... The American myth of a new and unfettered society in the new world never appeared in the Canadian textbooks."[1] Others have pointed to a less fulsome patriotism in a country with a non-revolutionary history like Canada. After all, Canadian history is pretty dull stuff—despite attempts by the producers of the CBC/Radio Canada's *Canada: A People's History*, by the Dominion Institute, and by others to suggest the contrary—when compared to that of countries like the United States or France with revolution in their blood.

There is, however, a quite different consequence for national identity flowing from revolutionary vs. non-revolutionary histories that I would like to highlight. It has to do with the way in which peoples who have lived through revolutions, especially ones that have had an impact far beyond their borders, come to see their place in the world, as opposed to the way in which those who have not lived through such experiences come to see theirs. To state things boldly, the former come to see themselves as incarnating a more universalistic set of values; the latter a more particularistic one.

Thomas Paine saw "America as the place to begin the world over again"; Washington as a temple of virtue; Jefferson as an "empire of liberty." For Benjamin Franklin, "America's cause is the cause of all mankind."[2] It is not surprising that the United States, with time, would come to assume the role of moral legislator for humanity. Walt Whitman captured this well enough in his poem about democracy, but also about America, entitled *Thou Mother with Thy Equal Brood*:

> Thou holdest not the venture of thyself alone, not of the
>   Western continent alone,
> Earth's *résumé* entire floats on thy keel O ship, is steadied
>   by thy spars, ...
> thou bear'st the other continents,
> Theirs, theirs as much as thine, the destination-port tri-
>   umphant;
> Steer then with good strong hand and wary eye O helms-
>   man, thou carriest great companions,
> Venerable priestly Asia sails this day with thee,
> And royal feudal Europe sails with thee.[3]

As for France, Jules Michelet, a leading nineteenth-century historian, argued in his *Introduction à l'histoire universelle*, "France reveals every nation's isolated thought. Hers is the speech of Europe, just as Greece's was that of Asia."[4] And a Minister of Education of the Third Republic, speaking at the inauguration of the Nouvelle Sorbonne in 1889, declared, "In the air that every civilized man breathes can be found something of France. It is not for nothing that she has given the world a double revelation: Descartes'

Discourse on Method and the Declaration of the Rights of Man."[5] France, in other words, was a beacon of reason and of political inspiration for Europe and for the world at large.

At least part of the American-French rivalry that has waxed and waned over the past two centuries can be traced back to their competing universalistic missions. There was a different content to the two great revolutions of the late eighteenth century, with political freedom looming larger in the American and the social dimension larger in the French.[6] The American model of a republic was pluralistic, forward looking, Montesquieuan in character; the French model was unitary, Rousseauean, haunted by fear of division and faction.[7] But despite these differences, the Americans came to see their model of life, liberty, and the pursuit of happiness as one with universal appeal. Think, for example, of Woodrow Wilson's proclaimed desire in 1917, at the time of America's entry into World War I, to make the world safe for democracy. And the French sought to extend the precepts of liberty, equality, and fraternity far beyond their borders, not only during the Napoleonic era, but long afterwards.

Notwithstanding their new world location, Canadians were a good deal closer in spirit to non-revolutionary states in the old world. Chateaubriand's observation, in *Le Génie du Christianisme*, held good for Canada. "Nations do not throw away their old habits the way one throws away an old garment. One may tear away certain parts, but there remain shreds that form an incredible medley with the new clothes."[8] The non-revolutionary character of Canadian development, unlike what transpired in the United States or France, helped shape the basis of national identity in Canada. Further reinforcing a particularistic version of nationality was the ethnic, rather than civic, character of identity that prevailed within both major language communities.

Where English-speaking Canadians were concerned, there can be no gainsaying the importance that a sense of *Britishness* had in defining identity down to 1945. To evoke a term that Anthony Smith, a leading contemporary student of nationalism, has helped make fashionable, I would argue that a majority of English Canadians saw themselves as constituting an *ethnie*, i.e., "possessing common myths of ancestry and shared memories connected to a homeland."[9] But the homeland in question, for many of them, lay in the British Isles; and its extension to Canada, even for those born in this country, was consecrated by Canada's membership in the British Empire. The Canadian poet Charles Mair has one of his characters (General Brock) voice a version of the British ideal in his 1886 historical verse-drama, *Tecumseh*:

> For I believe in Britain's Empire, and
> In Canada, its true and loyal son,
> Who yet shall rise to greatness, and shall stand
> At England's shoulder helping her to guard
> True liberty throughout a faithless world.[10]

For Colonel Samuel Hughes, the Minister in charge of the Canadian Militia during World War I, the slogan on the masthead of the newspaper in Lindsay, Ontario that he published, epitomized the British-rooted view of Canadian nationality.

> A union of hearts and a union of hands
> A union none can sever
> A union of home and a union of lands
> And a flag, British Union forever.[11]

An element of Burkean belief was in the air, seeing liberty not as some abstract idea linked to the rights of man, as the French revolutionaries and their supporters might have proclaimed, but as a specifically British trait linked to the slow, but venerable, development of English liberties. To this was added a racial element that linked *Britishness* to a sense of the superiority of the British race and of an empire on which the sun never set. John Seeley, a Cambridge classicist, gave the British imperial vision one of its more potent expressions in 1883, when he wrote, "Greater Britain is not in the ordinary sense an empire at all ... we see a natural growth, a mere normal expansion of the English race into other lands ... that our settlers took possession of ... without conquest."[12] *Greater Britain* was more than Great Britain; it bespoke an imperial federation yet to be created in an era of imperial expansion, with Great Britain in control of almost one quarter of the surface of the globe.

It was only natural for many of British origin who had settled what had become the Dominion of Canada to identify with this *Greater British* cause. William Canniff, Chair of the 1886 United Empire Loyalist Centennial Committee in Ontario, dreamed of an "Anglo-Saxon empire to cover the whole earth with the English language, English laws, and the English Protestant Bible."[13] George Munro Grant, Principal of Queen's University, sought "in the consolidation of the Empire, a common Imperial citizenship, with common responsibilities and a common inheritance."[14] For R.B. Bennett, a future Canadian prime minister, addressing the Empire Club of Toronto in 1914, "An independent Canada means that we Canadians are afraid of the responsibility and obligation of power, afraid to accept the responsibilities of our race and breed; afraid to think we are Britons."[15] *Our race, our breed, Britons.* There is no sense here of a differentiated Canadian nationality; to be Canadian implied a sense of racial identification with the British Isles, with its people, its customs, and its traditions.

No wonder Canadian immigration laws were so strongly anti-Orientalist from the end of the nineteenth century down until the 1960s. No wonder there was widespread fear among leading figures of the early twentieth century like Stephen Leacock or Andrew Macphail about populating Canada's Prairies with bohunks and members of mongrel races. The *Britishness* of Canada could only be threatened by the wrong kind of immigration.

Nonetheless, English-speaking Canadians, Durham Report or no Durham Report, had had to come to terms with the presence of French Canadians as a constituent element of the new Dominion. And for demographic and economic reasons, they had had no choice but to accept large numbers of immigrants "in sheepskin coats" from continental Europe. So that *Britishness*, a highly particularistic and racially tinged notion in its origins, would have to be extended to encompass a citizenry of more diverse origins, one less prepared to buy into a British-dominated definition of Canada. And there were competing paradigms of nationhood to the British imperial one on offer. Figures like Goldwin Smith or Samuel Moffett sought closer Canadian integration with the United States. Others, particularly in the aftermath of the bloodbath in the trenches of World War 1, dreamed of an entirely sovereign Canada.

Still others, whatever their view of the British connection, emphasized Canada's physical geography and northern character.

There is one further feature to the identification by many
English-speaking Canadians with the Union Jack and the British
Empire worth mentioning. This identification made Canadians,
from the time of Confederation onwards, conscious of functioning
within a larger internationalist framework. This international consciousness could lead to frustration with Great Britain, e.g., at the
time of the Alaska Panhandle dispute of 1903. It could lead to concern about where foreign and defence policy might be leading
Britain and the empire in the run-up to both world wars. But it
implied accepting the limitations of Canada's own position, and not
subscribing to an isolationist framework of its own. The Canadian
penchant for joining clubs (the Commonwealth, the UN, NATO, la
Francophonie, the OAS, APEC) may well have gotten its start here.

There was not just one dominant *ethnie* in the Canada of the
late nineteenth or early twentieth century. There were two. And
members of the second *ethnie*, the French Canadians, had a quite
different sense of their roots and origins than did Canadians of
British background. These different sensibilities would lead to persistent conflict between two particularistic visions, two alternative
visions of Canadian history and of the nature of the federation.

French Canadians traced their origins back to a different
European metropole—France. And despite the rupture with France
that the Conquest of 1759 had effected, the French Revolution that
had passed French Canada by, and the North American environment in which French Canadians found themselves something of
the French connection was to endure.

Hector Fabre, Canada's first commissaire in France—this was in
the era before Canada had acquired responsibility for its own foreign affairs—argued in a speech of 1886 that (French) Canada had
been formed in France's image. He also noted that if three million
inhabitants of Canada of British origin were naturally open to anything that bore a British imprint, one and a half million Canadians
of French origin were no less in search of what came from France.[16]
Wilfrid Laurier, on an official visit to France in 1897, made the following declaration: "Separated though we have been from France,
we have ever followed her career with passionate interest, taking

our part in her glories and her triumphs, in her rejoicings and her sorrowings—in her sorrowing most of all. Alas, we never knew perhaps how dear she was to us until the day of her misfortunes. On that day if you suffered, we suffered not less than you."[17] Olivar Asselin, a French Canadian nationalist and anti-imperialist who nonetheless fought for Canada during World War I, declared, "What makes France a unique nation in world history—superior to Greece in its seriousness and to Rome in its sense of justice—is its unflagging and profound reverence for ideas."[18]

This was one side to the French Canadian view of France. Another was rooted in French Canada's sense of bearing religious witness in the New World or North American continent to the universal truth of Catholicism. For Gailly de Taurines, author of *La nation canadienne*, "Our mission is to fulfill in America, we who are people of French blood, the part that France herself fulfilled in Europe."[19] For the Abbé Casgrain, an important French Canadian cleric of the last half of the nineteenth century, "When you have reflected upon the history of the Canadian people, it is impossible not to recognize the great designs of Providence that presided over its formation.... The mission of the American France on this continent is the same as that of the European France in the other hemisphere. A pioneer of the truth like her, she has long been the sole apostle of the true faith in North America."[20] For his part, Henri Bourassa, a leading intellectual and political figure of the first part of the twentieth century, spoke about the universal character of the Catholic church and of French Canada's intellectual and moral fidelity to France.[21]

Not surprisingly, there was little appetite in French Canada for schemes of imperial federation or, indeed, for the British Empire at large. *Au contraire*, there was a great deal of suspicion that English-speaking Canadians of the imperial persuasion owed their highest loyalty not to Canada itself, but to Britain. There was concern that, while French Canadians had seen in Confederation a pact between two peoples, too many within the dominant language community simply saw Canada as an English-speaking country within the British Empire, and were prepared to trample French Canadian rights at the first occasion.

Two *ethnies*, English Canadian and French Canadian, each with its own particularistic identity, coexisted side by side within the same federal state. Neither could entirely comprehend the other, nor could either will the other out of existence. They came to interact at certain levels, the elite level above all; they came, in some fashion, to develop the sense of a larger political community. Yet in fundamental ways they remained apart.

French Canada was a community defined by language, religion, and shared ethnic background, or to use the more common term at the turn of the twentieth century, race. One could draw parallels with the way in which other smaller peoples in Europe saw their fate, the Irish, for example, within the United Kingdom or the Poles within Tsarist Russia, Imperial Germany, and Austro-Hungary. To be sure, there was less of a sense of subjugation where French Canada was concerned; after all, Lower Canada had played an integral part in the Confederation Debates, and Quebec had gained significant powers in the aftermath of 1867. These powers did not negate a sense among French Canadians of constituting a community, nay, a nationality apart. And many were inevitably critical of the dominant English Canadian interpretation of Canadian national identity, with its strongly British and Protestant underpinnings.

Not that English Canadians, for their part, had a particularly flattering view of French Canadians. Many saw Quebec as a priest-ridden society, seeking to extend its tentacles over the rest of the country, especially the West. There was considerable animosity to the lack of French Canadian fervour when it came to supporting Britain in its growing rivalry with Germany. And when World War I broke out and French Canadian opposition to conscription became manifest, the vitriol of English Canadians knew no bounds. For the *Orange Sentinel*, French Canadians "enlist in retail and desert in wholesale." For John Dafoe, publisher of the *Manitoba Free Press*, French Canadians were "the only known race of white men who quit."[22]

What André Siegfried had called the race question in Canada (i.e., differences of religion, of social structure, and of outlook that divided English from French Canadians) was not unlike the linguistic and ethnic rivalries one found in Europe. Two particularistic nationalities dwelled within the bosom of a single state, each

Split personality.

28

rooted in its own version of the European past. Each had its own ethnic references, its collective myths, and its sense of an ancestral homeland on the other side of the water. What membership in empire was for the one, membership in a universal religion was for the other.[23]

Neither English Canadians nor French Canadians, apart or together, saw themselves as having the universalistic vocation that had marked the United States or France. The fate of Canada, like that of other small or middle-sized countries without revolutionary aspirations, did not weigh too heavily in the affairs of the world. Nor, for the first century of Canada's existence, were Canadians given to imparting lessons to others. English Canada for long remained firmly anchored to Great Britain; and French Canada, as it was called until the 1960s, more loosely but no less tenaciously, traced its affiliations back to France.

CHAPTER THREE

AS CANADIAN AS POSSIBLE UNDER THE CIRCUMSTANCES

Between the two world wars, Canada had begun to acquire greater autonomy from Great Britain. This autonomy was marked in the international arena by Canadian membership in the League of Nations; by the opening of Canadian embassies in Washington, Paris, and Tokyo; by Canada signing international treaties in its own name; and by the formal recognition of the self-governing character of the Dominions through the Statute of Westminster of 1931.

Economically, Canada had shed its reliance on British capital. Despite a short-lived attempt to revive imperial preferences at the 1932 Imperial Conference in Ottawa, preferential tariffs between Canada and the Empire were not a viable long-term option for Canada. Instead, the country was becoming a good deal more dependent on the United States, both for direct investment and as an export market for major Canadian resources.

When the Great Depression hit, it was to the American New Deal that many Canadians looked for inspiration. When workers in industrial trades sought to organize, it was American trade unions that provided the model. Culturally, Britain might still exert some influence, viz. the establishment of CBC/Radio Canada in the mid-1930s, inspired by the BBC example. Nonetheless, Canadian writers and artists showed an interest in exploring Canadian dimensions of social life or the uniquely Canadian landscape.

International affairs were another matter. Despite the claims of Senator Raoul Dandurand, speaking at the League of Nations in the 1930s, that Canadians lived behind a fire-proof wall, when war broke out in Europe in September 1939, Canada found itself drawn in within a week. And though the war helped to further Canada's development as a major economic power and reinforced Canadian self-assurance, it did not fully end the symbolic importance of the British connection. Well could the economic historian John Brebner observe, "In the deepest sense Canadians need Great Britain psychologically as well as materially. Few of them, except among French Canadians, could conceive of how they could get along without their principal sense of differentiation from Americans, that is, a sense of a nationality separate from the United States."[24]

Nor did the war erase old fissures regarding conscription between English and French Canadians. When the question of compulsory overseas service was put to the people of Canada in a plebiscite in 1942, the inhabitants of the eight English-speaking provinces at the time voted overwhelmingly in favour, but 72 per cent of the electorate in Quebec (and some 90 per cent of francophone Quebecers) voted against. Mackenzie King and his government were forced to manoeuvre with extraordinary dexterity to avoid wholesale political meltdown along language lines.

In the aftermath of World War II, Canadians became more interested in forging a new identity of their own. They were helped, in this regard, by the dramatic weakening of British power as a result of the war effort and by the subsequent dissolution of the British Empire. Growing immigration to Canada from continental Europe and beyond may also have contributed to the shift in national sentiment. In rapid succession, Canadian governments adopted a Canadian Citizenship Act; ended appeals from the Supreme Court to the Judicial Committee of the Privy Council in London; replaced British-born governors-general with Canadian-born ones; established a Canada Council for the Arts; dropped the term Dominion—too evocative of an earlier, dependent status—from federal government institutions; and adopted a distinctively Canadian maple leaf flag in place of the red ensign with its Union Jack.

This movement away from British identification should have led to a drawing closer together of English and French Canada. After all, it was the *Ligue Nationaliste Canadienne* of the 1900s, with figures like Henri Bourassa at its helm, which had agitated for a purely Canadian definition of identity, a pan-Canadian definition, freed of its British moorings. Five or six decades later, English-speaking Canada finally seemed to be paying heed.

But the muse of history follows a logic all her own. Even as English-speaking Canadians, by the time of Canada's centennial and Expo 67, were seeking a more self-confident expression of identity, one more congruent with the status of a core industrialized country within the larger international system, a new Quebec nationalism, born of the Quiet Revolution, had come into existence. This new nationalism, turning its back on the conservative values that had dominated French Canadian society for so long, was interested in the modernization and reform of Quebec. Successive Quebec governments, beginning with that of Jean Lesage, asserted Quebec's claims to greater taxing powers and to the full exercise of jurisdiction over various areas of provincial power, including social security. It was during the 1960s that the terms "French Canada" and "French Canadian" were consigned to the dustbin of history, as "Quebec" and "Québécois" increasingly replaced them.

The relationship between pan-Canadian and Québécois nationalism would prove to be a highly antagonistic one. It resembled the medieval theologian Nicolas of Cusa's *coincidentia oppositorum*, a coincidence of opposites. What appealed to English Canadians (e.g., a strong federal government, national standards and symbols, a more vibrant Canadian patriotism) would not appeal to nationalist Québécois. For a nationalist historian like Michel Brunet, "modern Canadian nationhood was merely a psychological equivalent of the British Empire invented by English Canadians to compensate for the empire's decline."[25] Quebec nationalists sought as vibrant a Quebec government as possible, symbols that were Québécois rather than pan-Canadian in character, and a revitalized sense of Quebec's national identity in which French language and culture displaced religion and race as quintessential markers.

What followed was a dialogue of the deaf between two opposing forces. The Canadian pole, whose champion was a federalist Prime Minister from Quebec, Pierre Trudeau, came to emphasize two official languages at the federal level, patriation of the Canadian constitution, and a Charter of Rights and Freedoms as the solution to Canada's national division. The Quebec pole, whose leading champion was the first sovereigntist Premier of Quebec, René Lévesque, looked to a Charter of the French Language (Bill 101), to a referendum on sovereignty association, and to Quebec's own Charter of

Rights and Freedoms as the Quebec solution. And though the federalist vision was to beat out the sovereigntist—by a fairly substantial margin in the Quebec referendum of 1980, with the narrowest of margins in the referendum of 1995—one would need to be naive in the extreme to believe that Quebec's status within Canada has been resolved for all time. Constitutional attempts at finding a middle ground, like the Meech Lake and Charlottetown Accords with their references to Quebec's distinct society, proved dismal failures. For the very symbolism surrounding the Quebec question prevents easy accommodation. What is a nation or nationality for a majority of Quebecers, even non-sovereigntists, is but a province among equals for a majority of English-speaking Canadians. Woe to the politicians who try to square that circle!

In the same way, the question of the status of Canada's aboriginal peoples has become more contentious and politically charged over the past couple of decades than was true during the first century of Canada's existence. It may be that the very vitality of Quebec nationalism served as an example for aboriginal peoples to advance their own claims to nationhood. Certainly the Charter of Rights and Freedoms, with its acknowledgement of existing treaty rights, provided enormous ammunition for aboriginal peoples to stake out land claims and advance other demands. A changing international context, more favourable to indigenous peoples, has also played a role. Suffice it to say that the aboriginal vs. non-aboriginal divide, complicated by multiple other divisions (e.g., across tribal lines, between status Indian and non-status, and between aboriginals living on reserve and those living off reserve), now frames debate.

The development of Canadian national identity has, therefore, proven to be an imperfect process. It sorely disappoints many English-speaking Canadians and a certain number of their francophone and aboriginal counterparts as well, who dream of a version of the American *E pluribus unum*. For the Canadian national project, if that is what it is to be called, seems doomed never to be fully consummated. Canadians seem to be cursed with the fate of Sisyphus, rolling the stone of the perfect constitutional agreement up the hill, only to see it come crashing down again; hoping to find in a common past—over which we disagree endlessly, for we have multiple pasts and diverging collective memories—the stuff of future resolution; looking for a great Canadian hero or lawgiver—a Solon or Lycurgus or Romulus or Aeneas—to bind us together for all time.

Maybe we have been searching for the wrong model. Maybe it is Europe, both the Europe of today and of the past, that more closely matches Canadian reality than the ever-present American model that many seek to emulate. For if we look across the Atlantic, we can find much that evokes the more complex national reality that is ours.

A number of European countries—the United Kingdom, Belgium, Spain spring to mind—encompass some of the same linguistic or cultural divisions that we think of as uniquely Canadian. After all, the Scots and Welsh do not see themselves as British in the same way as the English; nor do the Flemish and the Walloons—not to speak of the Bruxellois!—always see eye to eye; nor do the peripheral nationalities of Spain (the Basques, the Catalans, the Galegos) see national identity in quite the same way as other Spaniards. There are lessons in all this that we need to ponder.

Even more challenging is the process of trying to forge a common European identity. Charles de Gaulle, rejecting the concept of a United States of Europe beloved of founding fathers of the European Community such as Jean Monnet or Robert Schuman, spoke instead of "une Europe des patries." Margaret Thatcher, in her Bruges speech of 1988, made a fairly similar claim: "Europe will be stronger precisely because it has France as France, Spain as Spain, Britain as Britain, each with its own customs, traditions, and identity. It would be folly to try to fit them all into some kind of identikit European personality."[26] A majority of citizens in a number of EU member states, most notably the United Kingdom, Sweden, Finland, Greece, and Denmark, see themselves as citizens of their own nation-states first, with Europe as a distant afterthought.[27]

On the other side of the divide lie those who aspire to a federal-type Europe with more of a common identity. Politically, this was most clearly enunciated by Joschka Fischer, the German Foreign Minster, in a speech at Humboldt University in 2000:

> Fifty years ago almost to the day, Robert Schuman presented his vision of a "European Federation" for the preservation of peace. This heralded a completely new era in the

history of Europe.... Quo vadis Europa? is the question posed once again by the history of our continent.... Enlargement will render imperative a fundamental reform of the European institutions.... How can one prevent the EU from becoming totally intransparent...? [T]here is a very simple answer: the transition from a union of states to full parliamentarization as a European Federation.[28]

To many Canadians, this may sound innocuous enough. Federalism, after all, has proven an enduring feature of the Canadian political system, and it may be normatively appealing to Canadians to think of Europe evolving in a similar direction. But it is worth noting that only a tiny minority of respondents to Eurobarometer surveys carried out for the European Commission, 4 per cent in the EU-member states as a whole surveyed in 1999, define themselves as Europeans only. There is a larger middle ground, with 48 per cent of all respondents defining themselves both as Europeans and as citizens of their own state and 56 per cent of respondents feeling very or fairly attached to Europe.[29] Still, Fischer's federalist vision for Europe would be derisively dismissed by Eurosceptics, very much a majority in various European countries, as worthy of Don Quixote de La Mancha.

Perhaps the continent in which modern nationalism first took root will with time provide an example of how to overcome what Nietzsche in *The Gay Science* castigated as the *névrose nationale*. Perhaps the vision that the Spanish philosopher Salvador de Madriaga articulated in 1947 will come to be realized:

— Above all we must love Europe; our Europe, sonorous with the roaring laughter of Rabelais, luminous with the smile of Erasmus, sparkling with the wit of Voltaire ... where Hamlet seeks in thought the mystery of his inaction, and Faust seeks in action comfort for the void of his thought; where Newton and Leibniz measure the infinitesimal; ... their Europe must be born. And she will, when Spaniards will say "our Chartres," Englishmen "our Cracow," Italians "our Copenhagen," when Germans say "our Bruges" and step back in horror stricken at the idea of laying a murderous hand on it. Then will Europe live and then will it be that the Spirit that leads history will have uttered the creative words: FIAT EUROPA.[30]

Perhaps Mikhail Gorbachev's vision of "our common European home" will come to be realized, one where more exclusively ethnic underpinnings of identity within many of the different European nation-states will have been overcome.

But there is much in the European past that speaks to deep divisions—language, religion, imperial and colonial rivalries that have historically sundered the continent. André Malraux, writing in the aftermath of World War II, as bloody a conflict as Europe has ever known, suggested that "[t]he heritage of Europe is tragic humanism."[31] The German philosopher Karl Jaspers, for his part, noted the deep philosophical and ideological divisions that have characterized the European continent. "Europe is like life stretched between two poles, authority and liberty, political totality and personal domain, conservatism and radicalism."[32] And a contemporary American observer, J.H.H. Weiler, contrasting Europe with the United States, notes, "Europe is precisely not about one nation, not about a melting pot and all the rest.... Likewise it is not about indivisibility nor, blessedly, about God."[33]

It is no accident that Euro banknotes that are meant to embody a common economic identity and European space, picture stylized arches and bridges, but no specific figures or national landmarks. There is neither Rembrandt nor Dante nor Cervantes nor Kant nor Delacroix, to avoid the inevitable slights to national honour that would come from commemorating one figure and not another, one country's landscape and not the next one's.

Of course, Canada is a sovereign state, whereas the European Union most certainly is not. Moreover, there is a degree of shared citizenship in Canada that, for certain purposes, trumps the English Canada/Quebec division, the regional divisions within English Canada, and the aboriginal/non-aboriginal cleavage. Nonetheless, some of the same divisions that have marked Europe, not least those of language and culture, mark the Dominion of the North. And history is no more unifying a force in Canada than it is in Europe. For example, in a 2001 survey of history teachers in secondary schools in English Canada and Quebec, there was a striking difference in what each cohort held to be important. Anglophone teachers stressed events like Confederation, the two world wars, or the Charter; Quebec francophone teachers gave lesser weight to such events and greater weight than their anglophone counterparts to the discovery of Canada, the Conquest, or the post-1960 development of Quebec nationalism.[34]

In the early 1990s, the CBC radio program *Morningside* held a contest asking its listeners to complete the phrase: "As Canadian as...." The winning entry, emblematic of Canadian feelings of insecurity, read: "As Canadian as possible under the circumstances." This expression of identity, I would suggest, would also do very well as an expression of what the European Union, now expanded to 25 members, is all about. One could well imagine the winning slogan in an EU-wide contest reading: "As European as possible under the circumstances"—in 20 different languages to boot! Yet one doubts an equivalent sentiment, "As American as possible under the circumstances," finding much favour in any similar contest in the United States. Canadians, when they are so inclined, much like Europeans, can dream of a more perfect union. For the moment, and I believe for generations to come, they will have to make do with an imperfect mixture of languages and national identities that makes them who they are.

CHAPTER FOUR

MULTINATIONAL REALITIES AND AMBIGUOUS IDENTITIES

One of the signal changes in Canada over the past half-century has been the development of more civic, as opposed to ethnic, versions of national identity. As the British-based version of Canadian national identity that had dominated down to World War II receded, so too did the privileging of the Charter British group over Canadians of other origins. Access to post-secondary education, to the professions, to government employment, even to public office came to have less to do with one's ethnic origin and more with being a Canadian citizen, either by birth or naturalization. By the late 1960s, Canadian immigration policy lost its racially exclusive character, with a point system coming to replace a policy that until then had been overwhelmingly biased towards white immigrants.

In 1971, Canada adopted a policy of multiculturalism at the federal level. In 1982, Section 15 of the Charter of Rights and Freedoms entrenched protection against discrimination along racial or ethnic lines. So that, in theory, Canada has become a more ethnically diverse and colour-blind society than it was before.

Quebec too has travelled the road to a more civic as opposed to ethnic definition of identity. Replacing the "French Canadian" term with the term "Québécois" gave a geographical or territorial basis to an identity that had been essentially ethnic until then. One could be defined as a Québécois by simply living in Quebec; in the process, French Canadians living outside Quebec were excluded from the fold, whereas Anglo-Québécois and what came to be called allophones (i.e., Quebecers of other origins) came to be included.

Bill 101, as well, by ensuring that children of immigrants coming to Quebec would attend French-language as opposed to English-language schools, meant that French-speaking Québécois could no longer be defined as those who were "pure laine," i.e., of purely French Canadian background. Despite Jacques Parizeau's well-known jibe about "money and the ethnic vote" having lost the sovereigntists the 1995 referendum, the discourse of Quebec nationalism has become a good deal more inclusive.

Evidence of this can be found in a number of the contributions to a collection of articles on Quebec nationhood, originally published in *Le Devoir* in 1999, emphasizing the pluralist character of Quebec society and recognizing the importance of Anglophones, allophones, and aboriginals to the larger Quebec ensemble.[35] Although there is resistance to this theme by some of the contributors,[36] the debate marks a new turn in the definition of contemporary Quebec identity. Much the same is true for Jocelyn Maclure's claim to a Quebec identity respectful of minority nationalities and of the plurality of belonging. "Quebec-ness today is composed of many types of elements—past and present, cultural and intercultural, ethnic and civic, temporal and spatial, imaginary and material, local and global—and any attempt to homogenize that identity with the wider world or purify the difference within it strikes a frontal blow at the possibility of Quebecers seeing their identity as plural."[37]

Aboriginal identity is more clearly ethnic in character, stressing blood ties and tribal lineage, something that neither Canadian nor Quebec nationalism would do today. This ethnicity may account for some of the resistance that aboriginal nationalism encounters from non-aboriginal Canadians. For aboriginal identities, which are really an archipelago of identities rather than a single one, constitute a rather different tectonic plate in the Canadian national debate. Nor is the language of shared citizenship with non-aboriginals one that aboriginal spokespersons are always prepared to accept. Yet aboriginal demands need to be acknowledged, and within limits, negotiated in much the same way that indigenous identities need to be addressed by other European settler societies, e.g., those of the United States, Mexico, Central and South America, Australia, and New Zealand.

A key element in the relationship between majority and minority nationalities in multinational states hinges on the role that recognition and *ressentiment* play. Minority nationalities want recognition for their distinctive national identities, and are resentful of the way that majorities have imposed their will upon them in the past. In Canada, one can refer to French Canadian views of the hanging of Louis Riel, of the Manitoba and Ontario school questions, of the introduction of conscription during two world wars. As for aboriginals, there is much in Canada's colonial past that they see as oppressive. If we turn to European examples, we find similar patterns. In the case of Catalonia, there was the abolition of the autonomous government, the Generalitat in 1714 by a victorious Bourbon monarch in the aftermath of the war for the Spanish Succession; and for both Catalans and Basques, there was the suppression of their languages during the Franco regime. Scottish Nationalists continue to question the legitimacy of the Act of Union of 1707. The Flemish, although demographically never a minority, bristle over the linguistic as well as economic domination exercised by the socially superior French-speaking Belgians in the nineteenth and first part of the twentieth centuries. What minority-type nationalities want is some kind of recognition for their core concerns—linguistic and cultural survival, above all—and a significant degree of political autonomy to ensure that, in vital matters, they are not beholden to the goodwill of those who do not share their deepest concerns.

The centrality of language in the self-definition of minority-type nationalities like the Québécois, the Catalans, the Basques, or the Flemish cannot be overemphasized. A passage from an appeal by the Catalonian Cultural Committee in the 1920s brings this home: "Our language, the expression of our people, which can never be given up ... is the spiritual foundation of our existence."[38] In much the same way, two-thirds of francophone Québécois respondents, two decades after the passage of Bill 101, continue to express concern about the long-term survival of the French language in Quebec.[39]

The German Romantic poet Friedrich Hölderlin once wrote, "Language is the most dangerous possession, which is given to man so that creating, destroying, and perishing, he might bear witness to what he has inherited."[40] For his part, the philosopher Martin Heidegger observed, "Language is the house of Being. In its home man dwells."[41] Members of nationalities in multinational states who speak minority languages seem to live this experience every day.

41

Linguistic insecurity can contribute to a feeling of *ressentiment* towards the members of majority nationalities whose languages may have greater clout or international resonance.

Ressentiment is more than a matter of the personal pique that individuals experience when they become resentful of others whom they see slighting them. It can refer to something collective, to what has been defined as "a chronic feeling of affront, linked with vengeful desires that cannot be readily consummated."[42] It is not always easy for members of minority nationalities to avenge what they may see as affronts committed by members of majority nationalities at some point in the past. But if the opportunity arises (e.g., when these minority nationalities come to acquire greater political power, as in post-Quiet Revolution Quebec or as in the Flemish Region of Belgium over recent decades), there is little desire to show indulgence towards members of the rival linguistic community. Some of the politics surrounding Bill 101 in Quebec involved pay-back time for the Anglos who had lorded it over Quebec's francophones for so long; and the entrenchment of territorial language boundaries in Belgium and the simultaneous sundering of the University of Louvain/Leuven into two reflected the long-simmering *ressentiment* that Flemish-speakers felt towards French-speakers who had long dominated the country.

For their part, majority nationalities tend to identify with the larger nation-state—be it Canada, Spain, the United Kingdom, as the case may be—that demographically and politically they tend to dominate. They therefore fear that minority or sub-state nationalism may give way to secessionist movements. The idea of a Canada from sea to sea to sea is deeply implanted in popular sentiment in English-speaking Canada. The idea of an independent Quebec is therefore seen as the surgical equivalent of the removal of a vital limb or body organ. It would involve the Pakistanization of Canada, with a foreign entity dividing the Atlantic provinces from the remainder of the country. Nor would aboriginal sovereignty, a term that has been bandied about by various aboriginal spokespersons, win any greater favour among non-aboriginal Canadians. The implication would seem to be an archipelago of aboriginal tribal states, for the most part economically non-viable and politically unrelated to the larger Canadian ensemble.

How many non-Catalan/non-Basque Spaniards, for their part, would be comfortable with the idea of a Spain for which the Pyrenees no longer defined Spain's major international border? How many English would be comfortable to see the Act of Union completely undone and Great Britain ceasing to be an island-state? How many French-speaking Belgians would like to see their tiny state splintered into two or three fragments? Such sentiments can breed their own form of *ressentiment* towards the supporters of sub-state nationalism.

In the Canadian case, for example, there has been a good deal of *ressentiment* by English Canadians about official bilingualism at the federal level, all the more when successive Quebec governments have been promoting French unilingualism within Quebec's own borders. There has been *ressentiment* over the refusal by many in Quebec, unlike their counterparts in Canada outside Quebec, to see federal institutions and symbols such as the Canadian flag as national ones. And there has been considerable *ressentiment* over the efforts by successive Parti Québécois governments to secure the secession of Quebec through repeated referendums in which the would-be secessionists have set the question and the rest of Canada has had no say. These feelings help explain the strong support in English Canadian public opinion for the Clarity Bill passed in 2000 that sought to lay down tough conditions to govern any future Quebec referendum.

In the Belgian case, it is not hard to imagine the *ressentiment* that the phrase "Belgium Burst" must have evoked, the slogan of radical Flemish nationalists going back to the 1930s. Or how proponents of a Belgian identity would react to the claims of leading Flemish regionalists who argue, "Wallonia would do better believing in itself and building its place in Europe just as Flanders is doing.... The Belgian level is not necessary ... I am certain that there is no future for Belgium."[43] Endless linguistic conflict and constant challenges to the authority of central institutions have bred their own *ressentiment* among Walloons and moderate Flemish alike.

English national sentiment, for the moment, is more focused on the European Union than on Scottish or Welsh devolution. Yet the West Lothian question, as it has been termed, (i.e., the question of denying Scottish [or Welsh] MPs in Westminster a future say on matters affecting England, but neither Scotland [nor Wales]) is almost certain to arise if major additional powers formerly administered from London are transferred to Edinburgh (or Cardiff). A sense of Englishness cannot but follow on the playing up of the Scottishness or Welshness of the other inhabitants of Britain, and with it comes an element of *ressentiment* towards those who are not English.[44]

The members of majority-type nationalities are not prepared to play the historical villains of the piece ad infinitum to suit the interests of radical minority-type nationalists. Nor are they prepared to engage in one-way games of recognition with minority-type nationalities. Recognition must go both ways, they would argue. There is a common interest that weaves together Canadians and Québécois, Spaniards and Catalans or Basques, English and Scots, Flemish and Walloons—the ties of shared citizenship.

A related disagreement one finds within multinational states has to do with the degree of power to be vested in the central government. For the members of majority-type nationalities, the underlying logic is centralizing or, given the particular Canadian context, federal. The different units of the state, whether it is an officially federal state or not, should be seen as essentially equal. The central government ought to have important areas of jurisdiction of its own, beyond any encroachment by regional or local governments. Most importantly, members of majority-type nationalities see the central or federal government in such states as the national government. It follows that any division of powers of the sort that is common to federal-type systems is not a division between two poles of national allegiance. Rather, there is a single people that constitutes the common state, and the notion of the state being composed of distinct nationalities is profoundly troubling.

Most English-speaking Canadians have difficulty thinking of English Canada as constituting a distinct nation. By the same token, most non-Catalan or non-Basque Spaniards do not see their own national identity as separate from that of Spain as a whole. And in the British case, as one observer notes, "While discussion of nation/multi-nation in the British case frequently focuses upon Wales and Scotland (not to mention Northern Ireland), it is the nation which, as it were, created Britain [i.e., England] which finds itself most uncomfortable and uncertain in its national identity."[45]

For minority-type nationalities, on the other hand, the central government is not the sole national government. Many of its members have a sense of divided loyalties. Some may feel equal loyalty to the larger state structure and to their minority-type nationality; others may feel significantly greater (not to speak of exclusive) loyalty to the minority-type nationality. Data from cross-national public opinion surveys may help bring home the point.

Twenty-nine per cent of Quebec respondents to a 1995 survey defined themselves as Quebecers only; 29 per cent as Quebecers first, but also Canadian; 28 per cent as equally Quebecer and Canadian; 6.7 per cent as Canadian first, but also Quebecer; and 5.4 per cent as Canadian only.[46] In Catalonia, only 10 per cent of respondents in a 1992 poll favoured independence; by contrast, 41 per cent wanted greater Catalan autonomy within Spain; 33 per cent were content with the existing degree of autonomy; and 9 per cent wanted less or no autonomy for Catalonia.[47] In a 1995 British survey, 64 per cent of Scots and 41 per cent of Welsh respondents saw themselves as more Scottish or Welsh than British, or as not British at all. This was true for only 25 per cent of English respondents to a similar question about English and British identity.[48]

The bottom line for many members of minority nationalities is the paramount need to preserve the distinctiveness of their nationality. For those who are not secessionists or sovereigntists, this can be best achieved by maximizing the autonomy of minority-governed institutions within the larger ensemble. The logic that comes into play here is ultimately confederal, since it presses for something closer to a one-on-one relationship between the members of the minority-type nationality and the majority. And it rests on the notion that there are two (or more) peoples within the state, rather than one.

So there are often unrequited calls for recognition by minority nationalities within multinational states for their distinctive nationality and powerful feelings of *ressentiment*, on the part of both majorities and minorities, towards what they take to be the unfair demands or practices of the other. In similar fashion, there is a clear difference between those who think of a multinational state as made up of a single people and those who see it as made up of a number of peoples. In this all-important debate, the reference points for Canada are to be found in Europe—not in the United States.

If one took the examples I have cited to heart, one might conclude that it was game over, where the long-term viability of multinational states was concerned. Indeed, John Stuart Mill in his *Representative Government* argued that the existence of different nationalities within the same country, especially if their members read and spoke different languages, would make it next to impossible to have the united public opinion necessary to make representative government work.[49] The Canadian, Belgian, Spanish, and Swiss experiences would suggest that Mill was excessively pessimistic. For a degree of shared citizenship can develop, even in linguistically and culturally divided states. Where he may have been closer to the mark, however, is in noting some of the additional obstacles that a diverging sense of national identity across linguistic groups can pose for countries of the multinational variety. In such countries, ambiguity becomes a hallmark of national co-existence.

In Canada, for example, one has official bilingualism at the federal level, but a de facto policy of official French unilingualism at the Quebec level. The Official Languages Act and Bill 101 coexist, even though the logic of the one is diametrically opposed to that of the other. But as Galileo noted in another context, *E pur si mouve* (Nevertheless it does move).

Canada, in practice, is a multinational state with fault-lines of language running down the middle. This reality leads to the elevation of compromise into a high political art domestically. English Canadians must share their federation with French Canadians/Québécois who are less attached to central institutions or pan-Canadian symbolism than they are. For their part, French Canadians/Québécois must make do with a less developed version of nationality than might have been true had the British Conquest never happened, or the Patriote Rebellion of 1837 succeeded, or either of the two referendums on Quebec sovereignty held in 1980 and 1995 resulted in a victory for the YES side. Compromise may well be the name of the game when neither side can fully achieve its objectives.

Doesn't this sound a lot like the Europe that wants to turn its back on the excesses of patriotism that twice in the twentieth century brought it to war? It was Theodore Adorno, a founding figure of the Frankfurt School, who observed that Europe is a continent that has a great "tolerance of ambiguity."[50] For her part, Soledad Garcia notes that "modern national consciousness in Europe often involves fragmented collective consciousness as well as fragmented societies."[51] And Umberto Eco, observing a European Union with twenty official languages and an army of translators, argues tongue in cheek that "the language of Europe is translation."[52]

A new model of nationalism for the twenty-first century may yet turn out to be a version of "nationalism lite." Such nationalism seeks to be open to other cultures and nations, to a level of political and economic integration beyond the nation-state, to a global/cosmopolitan dimension of identity. This is increasingly the direction down which European countries, with their deeply implanted national identities and their divided and often conflictual histories, have set out. They are seeking to allay the sorts of hatreds that were on display during the recent meltdown of Yugoslavia and that still characterize ethnic and national rivalries in many parts of the world. Hence the moving statement by former German Chancellor Helmut Kohl when he addressed thousands at a ceremony in the German town of Zittau, which borders both Poland and the Czech Republic, on May 1, 2004, the day that the countries of Central Europe joined the EU. "The message is there will never again be war in Europe."[53]

Let us hope that Kohl is right. And let us hope that more accommodating versions of national identity, civic in character, tolerant towards other nations and towards national minorities, replace what Europe has experienced in the past. Such a model, I would argue, resembles the one that Canada has adopted in practice. For Canadians, because of the European-derived dualism built into their country from its foundations, have never known a seamless version of national unity. There has been lots of backsliding and resistance to accommodation at various moments in Canadian history. Battles over recognition have not been lacking, nor are they likely to disappear in the future. But increasingly, both English Canada and Quebec have become more open and tolerant societies, where the markers of national identity are less weighed down by ethnic or racial stereotypes, where there is more opening to the linguistic and cultural "other."

"Nationalism lite" seems to be both a Canadian and a European response to the experiences of modernity. For multinational states, be they Canada or Belgium or Spain or the United Kingdom, much like multinational institutions of the EU variety, cannot permit themselves the hard, impervious moulds of national identity that make co-existence across linguistic and national lines impossible. Theirs is the spirit of "live and let live," rather than of "my way or the highway." It is not that citizens living in such states or in an EU-type arrangement are more virtuous than those living in more unitary nation-states; they are not. But if the larger, ongoing entity of which they are a part is to survive, its inhabitants have to learn the arts of civility in their interactions with one another. And part of living together civilly in a multinational state entails accepting a significant degree of ambiguity when it comes to defining respective national identities.

CHAPTER FIVE

THE CANADIAN SOCIAL CONTRACT

Medicare has become a veritable Canadian icon, distinguishing Canada from the United States. At one level, this is a rather odd phenomenon, since Medicare has been around only for about four decades and was hotly contested—doctors' strike and all—when it was first introduced in Saskatchewan in the early 1960s. Moreover, the Canadian health system is facing serious fiscal problems. The Romanow Commission has proposed a series of solutions; and it remains to be seen just what the federal government and the provinces will be able to hammer out as their response in the years to come.

Nonetheless, there may be something fitting about the symbolic role that Medicare seems to occupy in the Canadian collective consciousness. For a program that Canadians think of as uniquely their own is in fact one that closely resembles what most West European states introduced in the post-World War II period. Indeed, Canadian social programs more generally help bring us a lot closer to the European model of the mixed economy and, in the process, to a philosophy of citizenship that stresses social rights along with political ones.

It wasn't always so. While Canadians were perfectly prepared to use the state, in John Corry's phrase, "to help build the playing field before the game can begin,"[54] this willingness had much to do with the hard frontier that Canadians faced, when compared to that in the United States. In other words, railway building or hydro-electric development or even national radio broadcasting were less amenable to purely private sector solutions, given Canada's sprawling geography, limited domestic capital, and low population density.

There was nothing terribly generous about Canadian social programs until 1945. Mackenzie King and the Liberal Party might have promised public health insurance as early as 1919; it did not arrive until the mid-1960s. Nor were Canadian old-age pensions a model for others; Bismarck's Germany had already pioneered such measures forty years before their arrival in Canada in 1926. Unemployment insurance, as well, was only introduced as a direct consequence of the Great Depression, and even then, not until 1940. During the New Deal period, the United States was well in advance of Canada in social policy.

The Beveridge Plan with its sweeping proposals for universal social programs, unveiled in Britain in the midst of World War II, had a dramatic impact on Canadian public opinion. And though the broad-ranging recommendations of its Canadian equivalent, the Marsh Report, were never introduced, the federal government did adopt an extensive Family Allowance scheme in 1944.

In the post-war period, Canada would begin to experiment with a more active state. With the 1945 White Paper on Employment and Income, Canada became the first Western country to formally adopt Keynesianism as state policy. By the 1960s, several of the more important pieces of the welfare state were put into place, most importantly Medicare and the Canada and Quebec pensions plans.

There was a pragmatic basis to Canada's adoption of such programs in the prosperous 1960s. Canada, Lester Pearson argued, could now afford these, when this might not have been the case before. But even Pearson, good Canadian Liberal though he was, let it be known privately that he felt most comfortable neither with the United States nor with the United Kingdom, but with the social democratic governments of Scandinavia![55] And his successor, Pierre Elliott Trudeau, adopted "the just society" as his slogan, further legitimizing a more activist role on the part of government in the social arena.

Developments at the federal level were mirrored at the provincial. Particularly striking was the change that Quebec underwent, with state coming to replace church as the central institution where education and social welfare were concerned. Quebec nationalist ideology, with its goal of *rattrapement* with English Canada and the United States, played a leading role in this transformation. In

Jean Lesage's words, "We need powerful means ... to put the French-Canadian people at the level of the present-day world. The only means we possess is the state of Quebec."[56]

The end result was a decidedly European turn in Quebec social thinking, with the notion of a comprehensive *projet de société* coming to loom large in subsequent Quebec political debates. It is worth noting, for example, that Lucien Bouchard, during the 1995 referendum campaign, made much of the argument that a sovereign Quebec would permit a more progressive version of Quebec development than federal policies would allow—this was the period of cut-backs to social expenditure in Ottawa. A likely future contender for the leadership of the Parti Québécois, Pauline Marois, has more recently reiterated the argument that the idea of sovereignty should be linked to "un projet de société progressiste ... un programme social-démocrate."[57] Such formulations would not be out of place in political debates on the centre-left in France, Germany, or Spain. I need but recall the comment by Lionel Jospin, the former Socialist Prime Minister of France, expressing his belief in a market economy, but not in a market society.

What is central to the European state tradition, as well-known British journalist Will Hutton has argued, are beliefs about the obligations of the propertied to society, about the need for a social contract, and about the centrality of a public realm and government to a happy community.[58] In other words, liberty is not a one-way street of grab-grab-grab, and social solidarity is part and parcel of what constitutes the good society. Accumulated wealth comes with obligations to others, and the public realm is more than a residual category for what the private sector overlooks. Without a fair measure of what another British author, Kenneth Dyson, calls "a disposition to approve of collective action,"[59] governments cannot play a compensatory role for the inequalities that markets, left to their own devices, engender.

Canadians are akin to Europeans when it comes to thinking about such questions. They have borrowed something of the spirit of Pascal, who notes, "It is not good to be too free."[60] They seek to find a balance between the extremes of the marketplace and the state, between individual liberties and group rights. They do not distrust government—although scandals like the federal sponsor-

51

ship one that nearly sank Paul Martin's Liberals don't help!—in the way that Americans instinctively do. Nor are they as blindly enamoured of the spirit of unbridled capitalism. A study by two American sociologists comparing two adjacent towns, Stewart in northern British Columbia and Hyder in Alaska, may help to illustrate my point. Canada, from their perspective, remains a more ordered, governmentally administered society than the US; by comparison, they see the US as a cowboy-based society, valuing *thymos*, high-spiritedness, over other values. "Stewart valued propriety, especially among the government officials who represented the town. Hyder exulted in its wildness and tolerated risk."[61]

Canadians, overall, have been more prepared to support redistribution through the tax system than has been true for their neighbours to the south. Much as in Europe, this attitude ensures that those at the bottom tier of society are better off, in terms of relative economic position, than tends to be true for their counterparts in the United States. Conversely, those in the top tier tend to do a lot better in the US.[62] For believers in a version of citizenship based upon social and not merely political equality, the Canadian and European model is the better of the two; for believers in trickle-down economics and the power of the market, the American model wins hands down.

The term liberal is not a dirty word in Canada in the way that it has become for many Americans. Not only does it describe the party at the federal level that has dominated the Canadian political landscape for much of the past century, but also it speaks to a deeper philosophical trait. Canadian liberalism has something of a John Stuart Mill/T.H. Green quality to it, believing in a measure of social provision so that individual liberty can be effectively exercised by citizens who might otherwise fall through the cracks. By comparison, American society has a more individualistic, contractarian, Lockean ethos to it. It tends to be stronger in its defence of property rights, and less generous to society's unfortunate in the process. To cite Peter Jennings, the Canadian-born anchor for ABC News: "Canada, as it is with some of the European countries, is trying to balance some of the market forces with public policy, which is not as apparent in the United States, where the pursuit of happiness and individualism are very much alive."[63]

One has to be careful not to go overboard with such arguments. In the trade-off between efficiency and equality, for example, Canadians lean a little more in the latter direction than do Americans, but only up to a point. Canadians have also been prone to buy into the merits of monetarism and lower taxation levels. I need but point to provincial governments like those of Bill Bennett or Gordon Campbell in British Columbia, Mike Harris in Ontario and Ralph Klein in Alberta, and to Paul Martin's 1995 federal budget with its steep cuts to public spending. (Quebec is something of an exception here, since attempts by the Charest government to go down the same path in 2003–04 have engendered stronger opposition.)

Nonetheless, Canadian social expenditure has not tumbled to levels experienced in the United States. Moreover, in a 1995 cross-country survey of 23 countries, Canadians were second only to Austrians in expressing pride in their social security system.[64] Michael Adams's assessment of Canadian attitudes in this matter strikes me as quite accurate. "Canadians, I am convinced, are pragmatic, not ideological, people. They want a sustainable social-welfare state, perhaps not the social democratic paradise envisioned by the Canadian left, but one which will still leave Canada a more egalitarian place than the republic to the south."[65] Or as British political scientist Andrew Vincent notes, "American patriotic sentiment, in general, cannot be doubted, but it can hardly be said to coincide with widespread interest in social justice or welfare.... In parallel, it is possible to have regimes with very low levels of assertive national identity, but with strong programmes of welfare and social justice—as in Canada."[66]

Canada is not unique in this regard. Neither Belgium nor the Netherlands nor Austria nor Denmark could be taxed with having overly assertive national identities. Yet their social expenditures are at the very top of the OECD rankings, whereas American expenditures are towards the bottom. Conversely, as is widely known, American military expenditures amount to a good deal more than the military expenditures of all the other NATO countries combined.

Canada may be a pygmy when it comes to military expenditures, and even the measures proposed by the Conservative Party would not alter this, but Canada is certainly no pygmy when it comes to social expenditures—much like the smaller and middle-sized European states. Moreover, this is where the two Canadian solitudes—or three, if we include aboriginal Canadians—potentially agree with one another. For each, in its own way, seems wedded to universally accessible social programs. And these, in turn, constitute an essential part of the Canadian social contract.

This general agreement regarding social expenditures does not mean that all is for the best in the best of all possible worlds. A fair number of Canadians—supporters of the Conservative Party generally fit the bill, along with those who look to the Fraser Institute or *The National Post* for guidance—would like to see Canada hue a course closer to that followed by Republican administrations in the United States. For them, privatization of crown corporations has not gone far enough; social expenditures and taxation levels remain far too high; and governments, both federal and provincial, are too committed to social engineering for our own good. NAFTA, if they could have their way, should bring about not only economic harmonization between Canada and the United States, but political and social harmonization as well.

A quite different set of challenges is associated with globalization, the buzz-word of our era, that speaks to factors—economic, technological, environmental, demographic, epidemiological—quite beyond the control of any one nation-state. Although sovereign states remain privileged actors within the international system, they are not the only ones. Nor do national boundaries today create the same high barriers to the mobility of goods, ideas, or people that characterized many countries in the late nineteenth century or the first half of the twentieth.

What does the increasing globalization of production and trade spell for social programs that, in almost all countries, including the European, are national in character? Can redistribution be extended beyond the nation-state, e.g., through major aid programs at the international level, or do we need to continue to focus primarily on the one arena where national governments have effective agency— the nation-state? The evidence to date is that social solidarity is a good deal stronger within national boundaries than across them. Even within Europe, there is little evidence that Swedes or Danes are prepared to share their social benefits, through steeply increased

EU-wide levels of taxation, with Hungarians or Greeks. So the social contract that matters most remains national in character.[67] But then citizenship too remains primarily national in character. In other words, the 1950 description by leading British social theorist T.H. Marshall of the thicker character of citizenship associated with social programs in the modern welfare state still rings largely true at the nation-state level, but not beyond.[68] Here, Canadians remain on the same wavelength as Europeans.

What kind of globalization should countries like Canada be supporting? There is a top-down version, fiscally conservative, corporate-oriented, tied in with the neo-liberal Washington consensus and with international agencies like the IMF. But there are also attempts to advance developmentally sensitive models, bottom-up in character, more open to the needs of ordinary people in the South. UN Human Development Reports are a good illustration of what may be required. Canadian thinking in these matters is by no means uniform, big business tending to favour the former, non-governmental and grassroots organizations the latter. Overall, I think it fair to say that Canadians with a developmental agenda, including many in government, will find a larger number of Europeans holding similar views than they will Americans.

Environmental challenges loom on the horizon, with global warming becoming an all-too familiar scenario through successive droughts, receding polar ice caps, and scorching summers. The countries of the OECD North are putting inordinate pressure on finite energy resources through their over-consumption. For example, the size of the ecological footprint, i.e., the amount of productive land an economy requires to produce the resources it needs and to assimilate its wastes, amounts to 9.7 hectares for the average American vs. 0.47 hectares for the average Mozambican.[69] Industrialization and rising income levels in the countries of East Asia, South Asia, and Latin America will put additional pressure on global resources. Yet it is the United States that petulantly refuses to sign the Kyoto Protocol, admittedly an inadequate tool, but still a step in the right direction. Here again, Canadians, though not those on the right of the political spectrum, tend to find themselves much more in tune with European thinking than with American.

Fiscal challenges also need to be addressed. Social programs are expensive and can easily account for up to two-thirds of all government expenditures. They are labour-intensive. They have their own built-in rigidities. The status quo is often an unacceptable alternative, if escalating costs are to be controlled. But if the goal is to reform social programs, rather than to abandon them holus-bolus, it is to European examples, from the British under New Labour to the Germans or the Dutch or the Scandinavians, that Canadians will need to turn. After all, much of the original inspiration for such programs came from Europe in the first place, and we should pay close attention to European initiatives in this domain.

Plutarch, writing in the early years of the Roman Empire, observed, "An imbalance between rich and poor is the oldest and most fatal ailment of republics."[70] This remains equally true for modern liberal democratic states. Faced with the extraordinary power of global corporations and the values that media corporations, so often in their thrall, project in turn, the challenge of maintaining equality as a core value becomes a daunting one. The same is true for citizenship in societies where the democratic deficit runs deep, and the consumer and shopper seem to have displaced the citizen from centre-stage.

But we need not despair. As long as societies do not succumb to the monolithic thinking associated with ideologies like neo-conservatism, in its own paradoxical way a kissing cousin to the Marxist-Leninist orthodoxy of yore, all is not lost. (For Marxist-Leninists, "collective good, private bad"; for neo-conservatives, "private good, public bad.") As long as a majority of electors remain attached to social programs of the kind one historically associates with the welfare state—something still very much the case both in Canada in the aftermath of the 2004 federal election and in various European countries—our societies can maintain a refurbished social contract into the future. But this will require a great deal of vigilance on the part of the Canadian public and an ongoing battle to ensure that Canada's version of the social contract does not dissolve into a branch-plant version of the American dream.

CHAPTER SIX

IS MULTICULTURALISM ENOUGH?

A prominent feature of Canadian society is the place that multiculturalism has come to occupy in public discourse. Multiculturalism is a relatively recent innovation, dating from the aftermath of the Royal Commission on Bilingualism and Biculturalism that was established in the early 1960s in the wake of Quebec's Quiet Revolution to address the conflict between French and English Canadian aspirations. While the major upshot of the Commission's hearings and report was the passage of the Official Languages Act, giving recognition to English and French as Canada's two official languages, the Commission also played a critical role in launching Canada on its multicultural path. Two of the original ten commissioners were of Ukrainian and Polish background respectively and were determined to ensure that while Canada might be in the process of consecrating two official languages, the same would not be true where two official cultures were concerned.[71]

The Commission ended up scrapping the concept of biculturalism altogether. In its place, it was prepared to recognize the existence of multiple ethnic or cultural communities, many of these with languages of their own, as part and parcel of the larger Canadian society. This innovation received official sanction in 1971, when Pierre Trudeau stood up in Parliament to formally proclaim the policy of assisting members of all cultural groups to overcome cultural barriers to full participation in Canadian society and of promoting creative encounters and interchange among all Canadian cultural groups.

The origins of Canadian multiculturalism, therefore, are rooted in ethnic communities of East European origin, concerned to ensure that their non-British and non-French attributes not be drowned out in Canada's pursuit of a bilingual strategy. I would draw an analogy, *toutes proportions gardées*, to the concern of many smaller European countries within the European Union today (not least the newer member states from Central Europe) that they receive European recognition for their linguistic and cultural specificities.

Canada's multicultural policy has undergone a number of changes since its initial unveiling. Section 27 of the Charter constitutionalized the preservation and enhancement of the multicultural heritage of Canadians. And the 1988 Multicultural Act acknowledged the freedom of all members of Canadian society to preserve, enhance, and share their cultural heritage. It saw multiculturalism as a fundamental characteristic of the Canadian heritage and identity and as an invaluable resource in shaping Canada's future, and it sought to promote the full and equitable participation of individuals and communities of all origins in the continuing evolution and shaping of all aspects of Canadian society.

Over the last three decades, there has been a dramatic change in the sources of immigration into Canada—shifting from Europe, which had dominated historically, to Asia and, to a lesser degree, the Caribbean and Latin America, the Middle East, and Africa. The 2001 census shows 18 per cent of the residents of Canada born outside Canada; and it lists some four million Canadians as members of visible minorities, roughly 13 per cent of the country's population. In short, multiculturalism today is a much more rainbow-coloured concept than it was, even back in 1971.

There is much about multiculturalism that represents enormous progress, when one thinks of an earlier Canadian past. It entails a re-definition of the national "we" in a more universalistic way, rejecting ethnic origin, race, colour, or religion as criteria for inclusion. It allows a larger place for cultural diversity within the Canadian ensemble than the older British or French moorings would have allowed. This inclusivity is very much the case for English Canada, despite resistance in some quarters to what is seen as hyphenated Canadianism, i.e., an emphasis on the hyphen in Chinese-Canadian or Greek-Canadian at the expense of shared Canadianism.[72] Cultural diversity is also increasingly true for Quebec post-Bill 101, though here as well there is no shortage of critics who fear, for example, that multiculturalism is but a Trojan horse for turning Montreal into a bilingual city, rather than preserving it as an international French-speaking one.[73]

It is worth noting that in a cross-national study for UNESCO of sources of national pride, Canadians were the most supportive of cultural diversity. Fifty-one per cent of Canadian respondents felt that citizens need not share national traditions, when the mean percentage response for all 23 countries was only 30 per cent.[74] The Molson beer ad of 2000 "I am a Canadian," contrasting Canadian values with American, also alluded to this theme: "I believe in diversity, not assimilation."

Some of this acceptance of cultural diversity reflects the pragmatic lesson of having to reconcile conflicting versions of national identity within the same multinational state and extending this to other cultural groups. In the absence of a stronger, overarching Canadian patriotism, it becomes easier for Canadians to accept the sort of diversity associated with multicultural differences. Indeed, there is a temptation to make a virtue of necessity, turning multiculturalism into a positive good in its own right.

The Charter of Rights and Freedoms has also played an important role. It can be argued that, with the Charter, Canada has caught up with the American and French proclamations of the eighteenth century, enunciating its own version of universal rights and freedoms. An important part of what makes the Charter distinct, in this regard, is its recognition of diverse forms of identity, including the multicultural characteristics of its population.

Canada has been an innovator when it comes to multiculturalism, since it was the first country—and is still the only one along with Australia—to have adopted it formally as state policy. Official multiculturalism can be contrasted with the policies of other western countries, e.g., France with its republican tradition, which was recently reasserted through legislation disallowing conspicuous religious symbols like the veil in the classroom, or Great Britain or the United States with their more pragmatic, liberal traditions.

In a striking way, therefore, official multiculturalism has given Canadian policy in at least one area a more universal cachet. It has led advocates like Will Kymlicka to talk about "the Canadianization of the world";[75] and Chief Justice Beverley McLachlin to express pride about Canadians "encouraging and nourishing the identity of the other, and celebrating the gifts of difference."[76]

Comments such as these, however, underline the risk that comes from overstating one's case. "Canadianization of the world" sounds dangerously like the hubris Canadians usually tax Americans with pursuing—"the Americanization of the world"—and provokes the suspicion that Canadian multiculturalism, in the minds of some of its proponents, may be caught up with a moral crusade to make the world safe for diversity, Canadian style. If so, it smacks of the same conceit that is associated with other universal credos, e.g., of the American or French revolutionary kind or of the era of European imperialism (British, French, Dutch, Spanish). Namely, it carries the assumption that one's society is a model that others should admire and emulate. As though the problems of ethnic or religious enmity that countries like Indonesia, Afghanistan, Iraq, or Nigeria contend with on an almost daily basis could be resolved by adopting Canadian-style multiculturalism! It would be a tad ironic, moreover, in the case of a policy like multiculturalism, for its advocates to show themselves so insensitive to deeper political and cultural differences among countries as to seek to export their model abroad. Here the eighteenth century French philosopher Montesquieu, with his recognition for the important role that customs—les mœurs—play in the affairs of different societies, could teach Canadian multiculturalists a few home truths. As Montesquieu wisely noted, what worked in Persia did not necessarily work in France, and vice versa. Has anything changed in this regard at the beginning of the twenty-first century?

There is also the need to avoid mawkish sentimentality when discussing multiculturalism at home. Canadians are not saints, and multiculturalism, more often than not, can become a matter of grand official pronouncements trotted out on public occasions to convince Canadians of just how wonderful they are. Are they really? Have racial discrimination or implicit preference for people of one's own background or for the native-born over newly arrived members of society entirely vanished from the workplace or from Canadian life at large? Do accent, colour, and ethnic background, not to speak of wealth and social position, really play no role whatsoever when it comes to making it in the Canadian vertical mosaic?

One also needs to ask, when push comes to shove, whether Canadians are not a good deal more monocultural than multicultural in practice. Do the different ethnic and cultural communities have very much to do with one another? Or does each community inhabit its own separate sphere, with multiculturalism being essentially a show-and-tell affair with limited substance to it? Intercultural exchange is not something to be fostered artificially—like the Potemkin villages with happy dancing peasants characteristic of Catherine the Great's grand tour of Russia in the late eighteenth century. It is something that needs to develop organically, through a bottom-up process of integrating immigrant groups into their new society, something that usually transpires over several generations.

Nor should we close our eyes to the dangers of importing old enmities, or new ones, into Canada as a result of conflicts overseas. The Air India bombing of 1985 by Canadian-based supporters of an independent Khalistan suggests that Canadians should be wary about giving lessons to others about our successful multicultural policies. When Greek-Canadians and Macedonian-Canadians faced off in the early 1990s over the naming of the Former Yugoslav Republic of Macedonia, little of the spirit of multiculturalism presided over their exchanges. The thwarted bombing of the Los Angeles airport in December 1999 by Montreal-based Algerian Ahmed Ressam or the fire-bombing of a Montreal Jewish school library in the spring of 2004 reminds us that deeper civilizational divides may well trump policies of multicultural tolerance within Canada's own borders.

Maybe, Canadians need to put some water into their multicultural wine and stop celebrating "the gifts of difference." Perhaps they need to be a little more hard-headed—a little more like the Europeans or the Australians in this regard—by emphasizing what core Canadian values really are instead of making of diversity an end in itself.

Canada is not a blank slate to be reinvented with each new immigrant or group of immigrants that arrives at our airports. Its underlying political and social values are ultimately European-derived ones: peace, order, and good government, constituted authority, political community, individual liberty, and citizen equality. Canada ranks highest in the UNESCO survey cited above for the pride its citizens take in democracy.[77] But the source from which this democratic tradition derives is Europe, and, more broadly speaking, the western political tradition.

To state this in no way implies a superiority for Canadians of European origin over those of non-European background. Rather, it is to emphasize the European underpinnings of Canadian society at a deeper conceptual level. The cultural and philosophical values that Canada has inherited from Europe have helped make Canada the kind of society it has become. And this remains true for all Canadians, regardless of origin.

To put things bluntly, I am not one who believes that official multiculturalism provides a satisfactory basis for defining Canadian national identity. It is something that works better in practice (i.e., on the ground) than in theory (i.e., as official state pronouncements with their tiresome evocations of the mosaic over the melting-pot). Nor should multiculturalism become a substitute for a sense of history and of the historical origins of modern day Canada; for a sense of our multinational complexity (English-Canadian, Québécois, aboriginal); for a civic consciousness in which ethnic, religious, or racial origins take second place to the things we share as Canadians; or for core political values.

Here the wisdom of older, established societies (e.g., European) may actually serve us in good stead, reminding us that identities cannot be invented *ex nihilo*, though they need to be recast to take new realities into account. It is not by taking multiculturalism to extremes, as some in the Canadian multicultural industry both governmental and non-governmental are prone to do, that Canadians will make a better go of defining their identity as citizens sharing a continental-sized federation and multinational state.

For example, faced with a crisis like September 11, 2001, we would not want to see the sort of thing that occurred in a number of British townships with large Muslim minorities, where fundamentalists stated bluntly that they were not British Muslims, but Muslims in Britain. If we are to tolerate religious expression and cultural difference, as liberal democratic societies are expected to do, we also have the right to ask those who benefit from this toleration to respect the norms and values of the host society. Minorities also have obligations towards majorities, or as the Chief Rabbi of

Britain, Jonathan Sacks, has phrased it, minorities need to be able to learn to function bilingually. In other words, they need to be able to function in relation to their own religious or cultural traditions, but no less clearly in relation to the traditions of the larger society.[78] If that does not prove to be the case, support for forms of religious or cultural diversity that are seen as incompatible with core mainstream values may well vanish overnight.

We in Canada need an element of civic virtue reminiscent of classical republicanism, along with the liberal and multicultural values that the Charter instils. We need a renewed sense of the importance of the public domain, and of the ordered liberty it provides, in a world where conflicts and crises of all sorts—civilizational, demographic, environmental, epidemiological, ethnic, political, religious, resource-based—are endemic. Along with multicultural practices, we need an open-ended form of patriotism—a civic patriotism that speaks to some of the elements of citizenship that members of our society need to share.[79]

What are these shared elements? Here are some: a sense of living together within a common geographical space in the northern part of North America and of wanting to continue to do so into the future; evolving political practices based on representative institutions of a parliamentary kind; a European-derived legal and constitutional tradition with added features of our own; an understanding of the obligations, and not only of the rights and privileges, that come from membership in a free society; and welfare state policies entailing a solidarity linked to membership in the same political community.

In short, I think Canadians could do with less emphasis on multiculturalism as a magic solution to issues of citizenship and with less moral righteousness when it comes to contrasting our policies in this area with those of other countries. Are the French simply being foolish to worry about the danger that Islamic fundamentalism in the townships surrounding major cities can pose to a century-old separation between religion and state? Or the British when insisting that immigrants attend citizenship classes and pass an English-language test as a condition of receiving a passport?

By all means, let us be inclusive in our definition of what it means to be a Canadian—something that has been the evolving Canadian pattern for quite some time, despite a number of shameful chapters in the past. But let us not make diversity a substitute for broader aspects of national identity or turn multiculturalism into a shibboleth because we are unwilling to reaffirm underlying values that make Canada what it has become. And those values, I repeat again, are largely European in their derivation, on both the English-speaking and French-speaking sides.

CHAPTER SEVEN

CANADA AND THE *PAX AMERICANA*

Almost from its inception, the United States seemed destined to play a leading role in world affairs. Despite George Washington's Farewell Address, disdaining "permanent alliances with any portion of the foreign world," Alexander Hamilton turned out to be the better prophet: "America would erelong assume an attitude correspondent with its great destinies.... A noble career lies before it."[80] Herman Melville, in one of his mid-nineteenth century novels, gives voice to the messianic dream underlying the American spirit. "We Americans are the peculiar chosen people—the Israel of our time. We bear the ark of the liberties of the world."[81]

Woodrow Wilson, author of the Fourteen Principles and the moral force behind the League of Nations, could speak about the hand of God "[having] led us in this way" and of Americans being "the mortal instruments of His will."[82] For Walter Lippmann, "Fate has willed it that America is from now on to be at the centre of Western civilization rather than on the periphery."[83] And for Bill Clinton, by the time of his second inauguration in 1997, the US had become "the indispensable nation."

All countries face the dilemma of co-existing with the United States, the hegemonic power of our day. This co-existence poses a particular challenge for Canada, a North American state, sharing the northern part of the continent with its powerful neighbour. It goes back to the period of the American Revolution; to the War of 1812; to the period of the American Civil War and the Fenian raids that followed; to Canada's involvement in the two world wars, long before American entry; to the Cold War period and American radar lines in the Canadian Arctic; to the contemporary period marked by the FTA and NAFTA on the one hand, and by 9/11 and its aftermath on the other. A good summary of the Canada-US relationship from the Canadian perspective goes as follows: "Ever since 1775, when the Americans broke away from Britain, we have had a love-hate relationship with the United States. We are both delighted and appalled by the US, often simultaneously. So conscious are we of the presence and power of our big neighbour, that the nationalism of Canadian people often seems anti-American rather than pro-Canadian."[84]

The alchemy of Canadian domestic actors in this regard merits brief mention. Big business, major farming organizations, and the principal media outlets are generally pro-American in their leanings. Powerful economic interests are on the line, making Canadian government actions that tweak the American eagle's feathers a risky undertaking. Moreover, there is support in right-of-centre circles of Canadian opinion for ideas like that of the Anglosphere, a loose alliance of English-speaking countries supposedly united by the Magna Carta and common law traditions.[85] Some of the strongest backing for American and western intervention in Iraq in the lead-up to that war and for Canadian involvement came from this quarter.

Those on the more liberal side of the spectrum in Canada, which would include a fair number of academics, writers, trade unionists, feminists, and environmentalists, tend to have a more jaundiced view of American behaviour. These were the groups that most opposed the Canada-US Free Trade Agreement when debate was raging in the late 1980s. They tend to be the ones most supportive of Canada's social programs. And their suspicion of American policies has grown by leaps and bounds in the aftermath of 9/11 and of the American-led invasion of Iraq.

After all, it was the Bush administration, with its hawkish worldview, that invoked a doctrine of first-strike, declaring itself freed from the normal constraints of international law and global public opinion. To cite its two principal advocates, Richard Cheney and George W. Bush,

> Weakness and drift and vacillation in the face of danger invite attacks. Strength and resolve and decisive action defeat attacks before they can arrive on our soil.[86]

America gained its own independence and helped free much of the world by taking on difficult tasks. We're a confident people, and we have a reason to be confident. Our Armed Forces are skilled and powerful and humane. They're the best in the world. I will keep them that way.[87]

The lead-up to war was a defining moment for public opinion around the world. The very public split at the United Nations between the United States and the United Kingdom, on the one hand, and France, Germany, Russia, and most other countries, on the other, was symptomatic of disagreement over the unilateral use of force. No less telling were the millions who marched in major cities and world capitals on February 15, 2003 in opposition to the pending war—the largest outpouring of political protest witnessed in modern times.

It appeared, at first, as though American power would prevail, despite the weak moral and legal position on which its case rested. Baghdad did fall within a matter of weeks, and the losses, on the Coalition side in particular, were relatively light. America, to some, appeared as a new Rome, dispensing its version of *Pax Americana* to the world. And the more arrogant within American foreign policy-making circles had little hesitation telling their audiences that the United States could dispense with the cavilling of its weak-kneed foreign critics.

Pride precedeth the fall. In light of the subsequent unravelling of the Iraq situation, it is worth recalling the observation by Goethe at the time of the Battle of Valmy of August 1792, when the Prussians were forced to retreat in the face of an army of the French Republic. "From here on and today a new epoch of world history commences, and you can say that you were present at its inception." The real cleavage that came to the fore in winter, 2003, as the French newspaper *Le Monde* rightly noted, was between two super-powers: the United States on the one hand and global public opinion on the other. And in this conflict, as Canadian opinion surveys were to show, Canadians at the outset of the war sided with the second and not with the first.[88] (It is worth adding, however, that ten days into the war, a majority in English Canada was inclined to support

Canadian involvement on the Coalition side, but with a strong majority in Quebec still opposed.)[89]

There are many reasons to explain Canadian reluctance to become involved in the Iraq war. Canadian foreign policy had rested on a tradition of internationalism going back, at the very least, to World War II. It had led to Canadian involvement in the formation of the United Nations and the NATO alliance, in the re-making of the modern Commonwealth, and in the creation of la Francophonie. It had resulted in Lester Pearson winning the Nobel Peace Prize for Canada's role in helping to end the Suez Crisis with the creation of the first UN Peacekeeping Force in Sinai.

A strong internationalist stance does not mix easily with the kind of unilateralist posturing that came to predominate under the bellicose Bush administration, "play[ing] by the rules of a Hobbesian world."[90] The Canadian position leaned more towards the Kantian sort of view that George Orwell articulated in the middle of a far greater crisis—World War II. "Either power politics must yield to common decency or the world must go spiralling down into a nightmare of which we can already catch some dim glimpse."[91]

Despite having come of age as a country during World War I and having made a signal contribution to the Allied war effort during World War II, Canada has been less inclined to support military intervention as a preferred option in recent times. In this respect, it has drawn closer to the Europeans, also less inclined to warfare, with Europe's dismal history of inter-state conflicts and overseas colonial wars still within memory. Canada, to use the pop metaphor, has come to resemble Venus rather than Mars.[92] Canadians show less pride in the military than do respondents in a number of other western countries.[93] "I believe in peace keeping, not policing," says Joe in the "I am Canadian" Molson Beer ad.

What Robert Kagan, the American neo-conservative analyst, writes about Europe would also apply to Canada.

> Europeans today are not ambitious for power, and certainly not for military power. Europeans over the past half century have developed a genuinely different perspective on the role of power in international relations…. They have rejected the power politics that brought them such misery

over the past century and more. This is a perspective on power that Americans do not and cannot share.[94]

Or as a former Swedish Prime Minister, Carl Bild, describes it, "Our defining date now is 1989 and [the American] is 2001. While we talk of peace, they talk of security. While we talk of sharing sovereignty, they talk about exercizing sovereign power."[95]

The United States, as the sole surviving super power or hyperpower, does not follow the same logic or constraints as other countries. As Ronald Steel observes,

> Unlike more traditional conquerors, [Americans] are not content merely to subdue others: We insist that they be like us. We are the world's most relentless proselytizers. The world must be democratic. It must be capitalist. It must be tied into the subversive messages of the World Wide Web. No wonder many feel threatened by what it represents.[96]

Mary McGrory, a *Washington Post* journalist, describes "America as [the] SUV of nations. It hogs the road and guzzles the gas and periodically has to run over something—such as another country—to get to its Middle Eastern filling station."[97] In Bill Keller's telling metaphor: "America is a feet-and-Fahrenheit power in a metric world."[98]

Canada also used to be a feet-and-Fahrenheit power, but it changed over to the metric system some time in the 1970s. Not without resistance, to be sure, from many in English Canada who saw the change as a wicked French plot to rid the country of its old imperial system. But change it has, by and large, with feet and inches surviving as units of measurement in plumbing and carpentry; pounds coexisting with grams and kilograms in many food-related venues; and Centigrade, litres, and kilometres displacing Fahrenheit, pints, quarts, gallons, and miles everywhere else. In short, Canada has been more prepared to adopt European and world norms in these matters, whereas the United States steadfastly refuses.

The same holds true, a fortiori, when it comes to American approaches to world affairs. The American doctrine of preventive war offends prevailing European and Canadian ideas about the rule of law and about the need for multilateral approaches in dealing with global trouble spots. It speaks to a binary, black and white view of the world when there are far more greys that dot the landscape. It has a messianic quality to it that, in an age of religious scepticism (at least in the West) leaves many worried.

To be perfectly fair, there was nothing uplifting about European behaviour in an earlier period, when European power was in its heyday. The Spanish in the New World or, for that matter, in the Low Countries; the British in India or Africa; the Belgians in the Congo; the French in Algeria or Indo-China; and the Dutch in Indonesia committed their share of atrocities and plundering, engendering bitter resentment among their victims. Compare the following observation in the sixteenth century about Spanish power: "I don't know what there is in the nation and empire of Spain that none of the peoples in the world subject to it bears it any affection."[99]

It is now the turn of the United States, having become an empire in its own right, though not all are comfortable with the term "empire," to bear the brunt of global hostility. For Iranians in the 1990s, the US was "the capital of arrogance."[100] For Latin American diplomats, the United States is irritating and contemptuous in its attitude towards others.[101] For a Czech graduate student, the United States has become "the new imperialist superpower that regards everything that happens in the world in the context of its own national interest."[102]

Canada faces the dilemma of living side by side with an imperial United States without being overwhelmed. It needs to defend *le droit à la différence* when it comes to culture, social values, and foreign policy priorities. The US is an ally for many purposes, one that Canadians think that they understand, though they are often fooling themselves. It is one thing to attempt to maintain a reasonably amicable relationship at the governmental level, difficult though this has proven to be under the Bush administration. It is quite another to simply pander to American wishes.

Concretely, the result has been to align Canada more closely with the Europeans. The fact that we are now dealing with a post-imperial Europe makes it considerably easier for Canadians than might have been true at the time of the Algerian War or the Suez Crisis. But the situation we face today recalls an earlier period, when

Canadian governments and public opinion might have looked to Great Britain to balance the strategic might of the United States. And it speaks to a telling reality of the contemporary world: when Canadian foreign policy differs from that of the United States (e.g., over the land-mine treaty, the Kyoto Accord, the International Criminal Court in the Hague, or the war in Iraq), it tends to find itself more in line with European opinion than with American.

Mistrust of American foreign policy has grown by leaps and bounds in Europe as a direct consequence of the Iraq war.[103] And the decision by the Chrétien government *not* to align Canada with the United States at the time of the invasion of Iraq turns out to have been the most popular foreign policy decision made by a Canadian government in decades.[104] It should help remind us that our attitudes on a range of foreign policy issues may diverge from those of our continental neighbour and that looking to Europe and the rest of the world to help counter-balance American positions makes eminent sense for a middle-sized power like Canada.

Foreign observers have occasionally remarked on the Canadian proclivity to see the world differently from Americans as well. Claude Julien, a French journalist who spent some years covering Canada in the 1960s, once noted, "Canadians are sufficiently conscious of their dependence upon the United States to actively seek out the presence of Europe."[105] William Pfaff, an American journalist based in Paris, has observed, "It sometimes seems that citizens of the United States believe more in Canada's necessity (as a non-United States American evidence of alternative possibility, demonstration of non-inevitability, even refuge) than do Canadians themselves."[106] Hanspeter Neuhold, an Austrian commentator, writes, "[I]n more than one respect Canada bears a stronger resemblance to the 'old Europe' than to its supposed neighbour. Similarities exist not only with regard to the positions on the use of force in international relations, but also concerning human rights, social policy, development cooperation and the protection of the environment."[107]

Perhaps the most telling aspect of this parallelism, where the *Pax Americana* is concerned, lies in a greater Canadian and European sensibility to the limitations of power. A German commentator underlines this sensibility, calling it "a basic insight of the Enlightenment, namely that human judgment and decisions are fallible by their very nature."[108] It is this fallibility that the Bush administration saw fit to ignore, landing the United States in the quagmire that Iraq would become. The US administration was prepared to believe its own doctored intelligence reports regarding weapons of mass destruction, to accept at face value the promises of exiles regarding kisses and flowers that would greet the Americans when they had overthrown Saddam Hussein, and to dismiss the importance of Iraqi nationalism in future resistance to any prolonged foreign occupation of the country.

Canadians, like Europeans, may be truer heirs to the Enlightenment. Or to put it more modestly, both have reasons to be aware of the fallibility of human affairs. The inhabitants of a continent that in one century experienced two world wars, two totalitarian ideologies, and the roll-back of extensive overseas empires know something about the vicissitudes of the political world. And Canadians, who have come close to experiencing political breakup in their lifetime and who worry about their survivability next door to the elephant have learned to forsake the world of simple nostrums for something more complex. In a post-Iraq world, a multilateral world that they cannot control by themselves, perhaps the Americans will eventually begin to do the same. But with a re-elected Bush administration at the helm, this is not likely to happen any time soon.

CHAPTER EIGHT

AMERICANNESS VS. EUROPEANNESS

In a passage that dates from the period of the American Revolution, Jean de Crèvecoeur, a Frenchman by origin but an American by adaptation, wrote, "*He* is an American who, leaving behind all his ancient prejudices and manners, receives new ones from the new mode of life he has embraced.... The American ought therefore to love this country much better than that wherein either he or his forefathers were born."[109] It is hard to imagine a Canadian penning such a passage. Indeed, as our earlier discussion would suggest, Europe continued to occupy a role in the Canadian *imaginaire*, both English and French Canadian, quite different from what Crèvecoeur—and millions of immigrants who subsequently followed him to the United States—would have acknowledged in the case of their new country.

To be a Canadian was to be a British subject until 1947, and even for several decades thereafter. It was, for many, to identify with the symbols of the very empire with which the Americans had broken in the course of a violent struggle. To be a French Canadian was to be a direct descendent of the colonists who had settled New France and to see one's community as engaged in an epic battle for survival as a French-speaking enclave in North America threatened with assimilation.

But Canadians—whether English-speaking or French-speaking—found themselves in a harsh North American geographical climate when compared to Europe, thrown back on their own resources, and far removed from old world conventions and norms. A rougher and readier equality would prevail in the British North American colonies than in the United Kingdom. This difference, in turn, would spark something closer to a love-hate relationship of its own. At one level, most Canadians were prepared to identify with British symbols and the British Empire until 1945. At another, one began to see increasing rejection of the trappings of the British metropole, e.g., *ressentiment* towards the snootiness often displayed by visiting Englishmen in Canada, the banning of British honours like knighthoods for Canadians by the 1920s, and a growing desire to hive off on one's own.

There was an "Americanness" to many of the original English-speaking colonists in Canada, a "basically optimistic colonial-American view" to their way of thinking that, more often than not, trumped the Tory sense of values among the elite.[110] This led as acute an observer as Alexis de Tocqueville to describe the British population of Canada as "identical with that of the United States."[111] And it led Lincoln's future Secretary of State William Seward, when visiting Canada in 1857, to see in "Canadians an ingenious, enterprising, and ambitious people" much like their American counterparts.[112]

Both de Tocqueville and Seward underestimated the peculiarly British character of the English-speaking population to the north of the United States. The latter sought the creation not of another United States, but of a British North America—British and North American at the same time. Their dream would come to fruition with Confederation in 1867. And it would fuel a continuing desire to remain a different English-speaking people in North America down to today.

Nor were the French-speaking inhabitants without their own peculiar characteristics. Even in New France, the *coureurs de bois* had not been subject to controls from above as was true for serfs or peasants in the old country. French Canadians were not just "a remnant of an old nation," as de Tocqueville had described them in *Democracy in America*.[113] They were also engaged in making a fresh start in the New World. Some of them dreamt of an Amérique française, combining French cultural characteristics with the reality of a New World quite different from the one that their ancestors had left behind. If the continent-wide aspirations that a number of nineteenth-century French Canadians might have had for their language and culture would ultimately prove a failure—though official bilingualism represents a modern-day variant of the idea—the desire to maintain a French-speaking society in the Americas has persisted to this day.

None of this "Europeanness" is to deny that Canadians have experienced their own fascination with the United States. Millions of Canadians since the time of Confederation, both English-speaking and French-speaking, have chosen to move south of the border. The Canadian economy, staple-based though it was and European-oriented though it may have been in its foundations, has become progressively integrated with the American, so much so that over 85 per cent of Canadian exports and close to 75 per cent of Canadian imports are now bound up with that one country. American influence pervades Canadian mass culture, from film, television, and music to the Internet.

The economic and cultural pervasiveness of the US, however, has not prevented Canadians from rejecting various aspects of American influence over the years. Examples might include (i) the Constitution Act of 1867 with its strongly British-based values; (ii) the creation of the CBC in the 1930s; (iii) the Massey Royal Commission on National Development in the Arts, Letters and Sciences of 1951, with its championing of state support for Canadian culture through what was to become the Canada Council; (iv) the establishment of the Foreign Investment Review Agency and Petro-Canada in the early 1970s; (v) Canada's refusal to join the American-led coalition in its invasion of Iraq. Canadian nationalism, to call it by its proper name, can also take more down to earth forms, e.g., the Molson beer ad of 2000 with its taunt—"It is pronounced 'zed' not 'zee.' Zed!!!"

At the beginning of the twentieth century, the Austrian satirist Karl Kraus noted that Germany and Austria were separated by the same language. This observation also works rather well as a metaphor for the English Canadian and American relationship. Canadian English quite clearly is not British English, spelling aside, but the Canadian accent is sufficiently distinct from the American, to Canadian ears at least and often to foreign ones. For example, in the mid-1990s, when China was interested in expanding English-language teaching through its broadcasting system, it favoured native Canadian English-speakers over American or British English-speakers because of the more neutral accent in Canadian English.

Smaller countries will inevitably suffer from a sense of inferiority when faced with a greater power beside them. At times, this feeling gives way to a form of *ressentiment* in which the smaller country's identity is defined negatively, as in the Canadian affirmation: "We are not Americans." At other times, inhabitants of such states can don the victim's mantle, e.g., Canadians seeing themselves as descendants from those on the losing side of the American revolutionary wars or espousing a sober Presbyterianism of denial to compensate for being overshadowed by their tempestuous neighbour. French Canadians have their own Maria Chapdelaine complex—*être né(e) pour un petit pain*, surviving in a world where strangers have come to dominate.

The challenge for Canadians has been to come to terms with their own particular place in North America. Being North American can open the door to a more capacious sense of self, to a future-oriented mentality, to a greater willingness to champion technological and scientific experimentation and individual endeavour. These characteristics are something Canadians share with Americans far more than they do with Europeans. They represent the American or, more correctly, the North American temper in the Canadian mind-frame.

Canada is a North American country, but the term "American," in modern English usage, has become synonymous with the United States. English Canadians, as befits members of the "other" English-speaking society in North America, have an ongoing need to differentiate themselves from Americans. Hence, there is a clear refusal by English Canadians to identify themselves as "American," though they would generally have less problem identifying themselves as "North American." Ironically, to add to the linguistic confusion, it is worth noting that in Latin America, *norteamericano* refers to gringos or Americans, i.e., to the United States!

In recent decades, a number of Quebec intellectuals and writers have been eager to embrace the term *américanité*. The term itself, as Joseph-Yvon Thériault has pointed out, can be ambiguous, sometimes alluding to being like the Americans and sometimes to adopting American material norms, sometimes used as a contrast to Europe and sometimes as the trajectory that all societies in the New World have followed.[114] There is evidence that *américanité* may have been borrowed originally from the Latin American *americanidad*, where it serves to contrast Latin America with the United States.[115] But in the 1980s and 1990s the term *américanité* in francophone intellectual circles often took on an anti-Canadian dimension, serving to contrast Quebec's supposedly more "American" character with that of English-speaking Canada and its pan-Canadian aspirations. In the aftermath of the signing of the Free Trade Agreement, the two solitudes seemed to be quarrelling over which was the more American, and which the less!

There are limitations to how far this argument regarding Quebec's "Americanness" should be carried. In an earlier period, Henri Bourassa, the leading French Canadian nationalist of the day, castigated the American worship of the golden calf.[116] André Laurendeau, editor of *Le Devoir* in the post-World War II era and an important French Canadian nationalist in his own right, argued, "The presence next door of the United States, a culture that surrounds us, weighs on us, infiltrates us, and has a large and rich population behind it, constitutes an immense danger. Faced with such a neighbour, Quebec is no longer in a relationship of one to two [as it would be vis-à-vis English Canada], but of one to thirty."[117] It is also worth recalling the significantly greater hostility of Quebec public opinion as compared to English Canadian opinion to any Canadian involvement in the American-led invasion of Iraq in 2003, suggesting that Quebec's love affair with *l'américanité* should not be overdone.

Despite the lure of *américanité*, the European connection continues to resonate for many in Quebec. "The European detour, part of French Canada's inheritance, is rich in socio-political lessons," writes Thériault, himself critical of the supporters of the *américanité* position.[118] "A true alliance with France represents a (cultural) counter-weight for Quebec and the sign of a certain maturity," writes Anne Légaré, conscious of the geopolitical influence exercised by the United States and of the dangers of a facile turning by sovereigntist supporters to *américanité* as compensation for their failure to achieve an independent Quebec nation-state.[119]

English Canada, to be sure, has its own strongly pro-American constituency, based in such organizations as the Canadian Council of Chief Executives and in the Conservative Party under Stephen

Harper, openly championing closer ties with the United States. Yet I would argue that a majority of Canadians, without denying their North American character, would like to keep a critical distance from the United States. And one important way of doing this is to focus more clearly on the importance of the European connection for this country and on some of the things that give the European Union a rather different complexion from NAFTA.

Interesting parallels can be drawn between Canada's position vis-à-vis the United States and Europe and the views expressed by Chris Patten, until recently the EU's Commissioner for Foreign Affairs, on Britain's position within the North Atlantic triangle. "... [W]e have, throughout our membership of the European Union, been confronted with a false choice between Washington and Brussels even when our wisest American friends remind us that we matter most to them when we count in Europe.... To borrow the jargon I am a pro-European Atlanticist. I do not feel obliged to define my pro-European sentiments in terms of anti-Americanism nor my pro-Atlanticist views in terms of anti-Europeanism."[120]

Canada, too, might best be seen as a pro-Atlanticist rather than an anti-American power. It is located in North America, but with important affinities across the Atlantic. Europe is more pivotal for Canadian political culture than for that of the United States, whose break with Europe was more complete. For Canadians, the European pole may even represent a version of the eternal return, in this case to values that helped make Canada the kind of country it was at its foundation and that, in transmuted form, may help to keep it on an independent path.

Europe continues to be a pole of attraction for large numbers of Canadians—students, tourists, artists, writers, professionals, second- or fifth-generation descendants going back to visit ancestral homelands. It is in Europe that young Canadians first began to put maple leaf flags on their backpacks to help distinguish themselves from Americans.

For it is when faced with "the other," that people often acquire a more acute feeling for their own identity. If this is true for Canadians vis-à-vis the United States—and even for Québécois, who are usually more comfortable with the label Canadian when they find themselves outside the country than within it!—it is also

78

true for Europeans. Two brief illustrations may help to bring home this point. "Personally, I feel most European when I'm with other Europeans in Japan." "The only time I feel European is when I'm in the USA."[121]

There is a need for Canadians to reflect upon our relationship to Europe in a serious fashion. We should be striving to deepen the relationship between Canada and the European Union, e.g., through cultivating more extensive economic, cultural, diplomatic, and scientific ties. Europe as a whole is one of the key poles, along with East Asia and the Americas, in an increasingly multipolar world that will shape the Canada of the twenty-first century. It is a major centre of trade and capital, accounting for 40 per cent of world exports and 57 per cent of world direct investment.[122] With time, the Euro may begin to rival the American dollar as an international reserve currency.

At the same time, Europe resonates for most Canadians in a way that no continent other than North America itself can. Not only do we have collective memories of battles fought there and of Canadian soldiers buried in its soil. Major Canadian cultural, philosophical, political, and religious traditions derive from Europe, influencing our very patterns of being. The old continent does not constitute a trivial set of influences to be shuffled off to the background while we focus exclusively on the United States.

Homer described Zeus, the father of the Olympian gods, as *europos*, as having vision.[123] Europe is a continent where visionary things carry great weight, along with things material. It is a continent where philosophy, theatre, religion, architecture, the plastic arts, science, music, and literature have flourished. It is where a concept of liberty, in contradistinction to despotism, first took root. A line in Aeschylus' *Persians*, the oldest of the tragedies that have come down to us from antiquity, describes the Greeks as "Slaves to no lord, they own no kingly power." The passage is symptomatic of a deeper European political outlook.

Europe has been the source of ideas about freedom, justice, liberty, and political regimes; the progenitor of the cosmopolitan idea, from the time of the Stoics down to modern times,[124] at the origins of the utopian idea.[125] It is also, *faute de mieux*, the source of the modern pluralist ideal. For Agnes Heller, "What has been designated as a possible European culture is not meant as a merger of cultures—more of a loss than a gain—rather, it is meant as a new lay umbrella culture in whose framework local, partial, and national cultures may thrive."[126] For Michael Greven, "Despite the fact that European nation-states share, in a very broad sense, a common European historical and cultural heritage, they are also home to a diverse array of cultures in general, and political cultures in particular."[127]

Nonetheless, the idea of Europe has spawned a more precise sense of identity than what one finds on other continents.[128] For example, if one compares the European Union with NAFTA, one finds that NAFTA is essentially a free trade arrangement with little resonance at the level of the popular imagination. Business and political elites pushed the case for North American economic integration; there has been a good deal less by way of intellectual championing of this idea or of grass-roots support for political or cultural integration at the continental level.

The political reasons for this are pretty straightforward. So great is American hegemony within the continent that NAFTA's two other members, Canada and Mexico, would have every reason to fear the consequences of a North American Union resembling the EU. Nor would the American Congress consider for one moment surrendering the levers of power that rest so firmly within the United States to a supranational organization. The shades of manifest destiny are too powerful to allow that.

Cultural factors are also quite important. For all the geographical features that may link Canada, the United States, and Mexico, there is less sense of a common North Americanness when it comes to culture. If Latin Americans can sometimes evoke *nuestra America*, North Americans rarely do the same. There are language barriers—Spanish in the case of Mexico and French in the case of Quebec—to impede such a common quest, though it is worth noting that the far more numerous languages of Europe do not seem to stand in the way of the search for a common Europeanness. There is less sense of a single North American space, partly because of the very size of the continent, and partly because the three states of North America, unlike their European counterparts, are all relatively new, without the legacy of Mediterranean civilizations, the Roman Empire, or a medieval past to summon up. There is also relatively little emphasis on common North American features, as opposed to distinctly national ones, when it comes to thinking about their different histories.

In Europe, history can never be purely national, if only because the proximity of countries and linguistic groups to one another ensured a great deal of interaction, commerce, warfare, and population exchange through the centuries. A European dimension has therefore sprung up alongside the more purely national. This doesn't mean that the European pole trumps the latter—*tout au contraire*. But it helps provide a richer cultural foundation for the European Union than NAFTA can ever have.

In today's European Union with its 25 members, no single country can dominate. True, during its first forty years, the French-German locomotive provided the principal momentum for European construction. This engine may prove more difficult to duplicate in the future. The European Union, however, rests on more than economic foundations. The idea of Europe—contested though it may be, buffeted by divergent and often contradictory historical memories—is sufficiently rooted in a broader European past, including the older Latin-based republic of letters, to pack significant normative appeal. And the desire to transcend the negative parts of that past, e.g., the barbarism that all too often has been engendered along the way, also explains a greater willingness to espouse a form of common European identity today.

It might be useful to list some of the core values that the preamble to the European constitution contains. These include equality of persons, freedom, and respect for reason; inspiration from [Europe's] cultural, religious, and humanist inheritance; respect for law; deepening the democratic nature of public life; prosperity for all [of Europe's] inhabitants, including its weakest and most deprived; and unity in its diversity.[129]

Whatever the ultimate fate of this particular document—and its ratification still hangs very much in the balance—its compilation of European values reminds us that the raison d'être behind the European Union taps into multifaceted cultural, historical, and philosophical traditions on which contemporary Europe can build. And it provides an opening for a different kind of politics from what has prevailed in the United States in recent years.

A short excerpt from a statement made at the time of the European Parliamentary Elections of June 2004 by Pat Cox, the outgoing President of the European Parliament, may help to further reinforce this political difference.

> If you look at law-making in this parliament, much ... of it is about sustainability and the environment.... To give Europe real meaning, we must talk about the values of pluralist democracy which underpin the European Union. It is not by accident that Spain joined after Franco, Portugal after Salazar, Greece after the Colonels and now the states of Central and Eastern Europe after the collapse of the Soviet Empire.... We must talk to people about human rights and the rule of law. I am proud that Europe led the way on setting up the International Criminal Court to fight for international human rights. I would prefer any day the due process of an ICC to the absence of process in Guantanamo Bay and elsewhere. And talk about our values of solidarity and cohesion. Even though we could do more, the European Union is the largest donor community of aid to the poorest countries on earth—outspending the USA by two-and-a-half to one every year in untied official assistance.[130]

The United States may be next door, and Europe an ocean away. But Canadians are heirs to the same core European values that the preamble to the European constitution outlines; and many would feel considerable affinity with the positions that Pat Cox has outlined for Europe. The moral of the story seems clear enough. It is not by denying their European roots that Canadians can best define themselves. Rather, it is through maintaining an ongoing dialogue between their "(North) Americanness" and their "Europeanness," today as in the past, that they can best foster their own sense of identity.

CHAPTER NINE

THE CULTURAL IMPERATIVE

Towards the dawn of the Cold War, Harold Innis, the distinguished Canadian economic historian, argued, "We can only survive by taking persistent action at strategic points against American imperialism in all its attractive guises."[131] Innis was prepared to see the United States in a way that most of his compatriots at the time were not—as the seat of a powerful and overweening empire. But there were many things attractive about the American empire (unlike say the Soviet) that made it a more difficult force to resist.

Perhaps the single greatest danger came from homogenisation—the American way of life acting as an economic and cultural juggernaut rolling over everything that stands in its way. This danger explains why the debate over American ownership of the Canadian economy was such a passionate one in the 1960s, spilling over into questions of university recruitment, Canadian magazine content, and much besides. It explains why the Free Trade Agreement so dominated the 1988 federal election, leading many of its opponents to believe (incorrectly as it turned out) that its ratification might in fact signal the demise of Canada. The FTA and NAFTA have certainly brought about a more rapid integration of the two economies than before. They have contributed to pressures for harmonizing Canadian taxation policy with American—something that could, in the long run, spell real trouble for the financing of Canadian social programs. But to date they have not brought about the wholesale erosion of distinctive Canadian values.

Michael Adams has provided some useful survey data in his book *Fire and Ice* to illustrate why this erosion has not happened until now. The data show that on a range of issues—from the authority of the father in the family, to a laissez-faire approach to government, to religious practice, to civic engagement, to claims of national superiority, to the quest for fulfilment—Canadians differ profoundly from Americans.[132]

What needs to be emphasized, in addition, is just how much closer in terms of important core values Canadians are to today's Europeans. The most striking example of this may well be on questions of religion, where a battery of evidence now points to the outrider character of American beliefs. Seymour Martin Lipset, in his pioneering study *Continental Divide*, saw greater fundamentalism in American religious life by the 1960s; Canadian churches, by comparison, were more ecumenical and communitarian.[133] A more recent study by sociologists Neil MacKinnon and Alison Luke pointed to the growing secularisation of Canadian society between 1981 and 1995. There was a general decline in the status and power of religious identities such as clergyman, evangelist, and even God. Moreover, only a relatively small minority of young Canadians aged between 15 and 24 indicated that they valued religion in their everyday lives.[134]

Nietzsche's *Thus Spake Zarathustra* first sounded the tocsin announcing the imminent decline of religion. Julian Young has argued that European continental philosophy of the twentieth century more generally has been marked by the death of god and by the search for meaning.[135] Nietzsche, Heidegger, Sartre, and Camus are some of the more important contributors to this tradition, one that has now become very much a majority credo among Europeans at large. Eloquent proof of the decline of religion in Europe was contained in a Pew survey of global public opinion canvassing 38,000 respondents on different continents, which was released in December 2002. Fully 59 per cent of American respondents claimed that religion played a very important role in their lives compared to 30 per cent of Canadians responding in the same manner. The response from Europe showed 11 per cent in France, 21 per cent in Germany, and 27 per cent in Italy saying that religion was very important to them. The director of the Washington-based survey, Andrew Kohut, is quoted as saying, "The survey shows that Americans are more religious than people in other developed countries, even those who are so culturally similar to us in so many other ways. Americans still believe they are one nation under God, whereas Europe is becomingly increasingly secular."[136]

Fundamentalism represents a powerful streak in American political culture. Before his 2000 campaign, George W. Bush confided to a leader of the religious right, "I feel like God wants me to run for president … I sense my country is going to need me. Something is going to happen."[137] It is estimated that there are 90 million evangelical Christians in the US and that 59 per cent of Americans trust that St. John's prophecies foretold in the Book of Revelations will be fulfilled—probably during their lifetime.[138] By comparison, fundamentalists make up no more than 10 per cent of the Canadian population.[139] Indeed, in a province like British Columbia, fully 35 per cent of the population, according to the 2001 Canadian Census, profess no religious faith whatsoever. And in Quebec, ever since the Quiet Revolution, Church adherence and influence have been in free-fall.

When it comes to religious practice, therefore, Canada resembles Europe more than it does the United States. Canada, once the more conservative of the two North American states and closer to Europe as a result, is today the more secular of the two societies and, in today's context, the more European. The same applies to other issues (e.g., abolition of the death penalty, access to abortion, legalization of marijuana, gay marriage) where again Canadian views tend to be closer to those of Europeans.

How much does the European connection provide a unifying explanation for this phenomenon? It played a role when it came to explaining the presence of Toryism and social democracy alongside liberalism in earlier Canadian political culture. After all, Canadian political parties closely resembled those of Great Britain, as did the ideological range of views to be found in Canadian political debate.

Should one today lay emphasis on common western values spanning the Atlantic? On post-materialism, as some have argued? On an ingrained Canadian willingness to look to the outside world, going back to our colonial past? The fact remains that Canadians continue to react in a more European way to some of modernity's challenges—and this despite the enormous influence that the United States exercises over our daily lives.

Canadian party politics is an illustration of this. Judging from the 2004 federal election results, 37 per cent of Canadian voters identify with the Liberals; 30 per cent with the Conservatives; 28 per cent with a social democratic current, split between the NDP in English Canada and the sovereigntist Bloc Québécois in Quebec; and 4 per cent with the Greens. This multi-party constellation with its spectrum of views from right to left, including Quebec sovereigntists, aligns Canadian political culture fairly closely to prevailing European norms. (See, for example, the range of parties, including anti-EU ones, represented in the current European Parliament.) By comparison, the American political spectrum, as the 2004 Presidential and Congressional elections confirm, is 10 to 15 degrees further to the right than either the Canadian or the European, and less fissiparous in character. In the words of former US ambassador to France Felix Rohatyn, "[The United States] is more individualistic than Europe, more religious, conservative and patriotic ... [These factors] will influence everything America does from now on, both in its foreign and its domestic policies."[140]

A further illustration of Canadian-European parallelism lies in the importance that culture has assumed in public life. Jean Monnet, one of the key architects of European unification, allowed himself the following reflection towards the end of a long career: "If I should start it all over again, I would start with culture." That seems to be where Canadians have chosen to draw the line with regards to their own special relationship with the United States.

Culture was formally exempted from the Free Trade Agreement, despite penalties written into the Agreement for crossing American interests on this score. The potent opposition of members of Canada's cultural community to the Agreement certainly had something to do with this exemption. Like the Europeans, Canada has for long used cultural subsidies as a crucial element of cultural policy. In the late-1990s, Canada found itself allied with France in opposing the Multilateral Agreement on Investments that had been negotiated through the OECD; the defence of cultural diversity was central to their common stand. What Antonio Muñoz Molina, a Spanish writer, argues in this regard could apply to Canada just as well. "In Europe, unlike the United States, there is a consensus that culture is a public good much like education and health, that cannot be left to the strict laws of the market."[141]

Highlighting the values we share with Europeans becomes in our day and age a way of asserting a uniquely Canadian way of life in

North America. It can also have the beneficial side effect of helping to reinforce internal Canadian unity, or at least mutual comprehension. For both English Canadians and Québécois have reasons to look to Europe as a source of civilizational support in their attempt to shore up their continued existence as distinct societies.

André Laurendeau and Marcel Rioux were heralds of the sort of deeper understanding between anglophones and francophones that I have in mind. For Laurendeau, "The homogenizing influence of the United States puts into question the very existence of both Canadian cultures [i.e., English and French]. Faced with this mortal danger, we in Canada must develop a friendship between our two cultures."[142] For Rioux, writing at the time of the Free Trade Agreement, "Today, when the Americans, who long ago replaced the British, are in the process of completing their domination of Quebec and Canada through treaties, Québécois foolishly refuse to see a thing…. It is as though Upper Canada remains the enemy."[143]

It behoves us to pick up on Laurendeau's and Rioux's challenge. Effective collaboration between English Canadians and Québécois is vital in trying to fend off American cultural and ideological domination. This cooperation can only take place within a context that respects cultural pluralism and differing perspectives on national identity—what Charles Taylor has termed deep diversity. But it can occur.

I would draw an analogy with the *entente cordiale* between France and Great Britain whose centenary was recently celebrated. While the two have not fought each other for over a hundred years, it has not been all love and kisses between the two countries, as their opposing policies at the time of the Iraq War would underline. Still, the two are forced to co-operate together within the EU, much as their offshoots within Canada find themselves forced to cohabit and co-operate with one another.

Emphasizing the shared European elements of Canadian identity represents a more positive way of meeting the challenge of American domination than George Grant's lament for a nation or the Parti Québécois' sovereigntist dream, for it speaks to something that can unite the two solitudes in a way that support for the British Empire during Canada's long apprenticeship years as a Dominion or General de Gaulle's "Vive le Québec libre" cry, with its backward-looking appeal to *les Français d'Amérique*, never could. Are Canadians and Québécois up to recognizing the potentially new element that European integration introduces into the long-running internal Canadian debate? We are no longer being asked to choose with which of the European mother countries (Great Britain or France) we should identify. Europe is a kaleidoscope of cultures, not unlike Canada. And the EU, mercy be, does not solicit our emotional attachment! The EU, for all its internal disagreements and limitations, can, however, help provide Canada with a counter-weight to American hegemony in a world where American values, in a number of telling respects, differ from our own. Can China provide an equivalent counter-weight? Or Japan? Or Latin America? I rather doubt it. As the philosopher Slavoj Zizek has argued, "The Third World cannot generate a strong enough resistance to the ideology of the American Dream; in the present constellation, it is only Europe that can do it."[144]

Where Claude Julien once wrote about Canada being Europe's last chance, it might be more appropriate to suggest that Europe is Canada's last chance to pursue more progressive, open-ended policies than those of the United States, and this in a multilateral context. The French newspaper *Le Monde*, in the immediate aftermath of September 11, 2001, stated in a much commented upon editorial, "We are all Americans." Most Canadians felt solidarity with the Americans in their moment of affliction, as did most Europeans. In the spring of 2004, in the aftermath of the American War on Terror and the prison atrocities at Abu Ghraib, *Le Monde* penned another editorial, "We are all not Americans."[145] We need some of that same critical backbone in Canada if we are to successfully resist the naked blandishments of American power. Europe represents not so much an effective economic alternative to the United States as a cultural and political counter-model for both Canada and Quebec in the age of the American empire.

CHAPTER TEN

THE METAPHYSICS
OF CANADIAN IDENTITY

As I have argued in the course of this essay, a number of elements go into the making of Canadian identity. These include European historical connections, a North American geographical setting, multiple national identities, robust social programs, multicultural practices, increasingly secular values, and a multilateral outlook on international affairs.

However, what is the dominant motif in Canadian political culture, the one that more than any other sets it off from its American counterpart? That element, I am tempted to argue, is self-doubt. Doubt about who we are—one or many, solidaristic or apart. About the ultimate purpose behind the Canadian experiment. About the very possibility of summing up the Canadian identity puzzle. Doubt about Canada's place on the North American continent and in the larger world.

This doubt has historic roots. French Canadians, whose ties with the original metropole were severed after 1759, had to adjust to the reality of new colonial masters and subsequently to the status of being a permanent national minority within the larger Canadian framework. Theirs was often the melancholy associated with small nations, whose dreams of a lost past and of a different future have been hopelessly dashed.[146] Theirs were the inward-looking, national preoccupations that István Bibó had ascribed to central European states and that Pierre Trudeau had castigated in one of his earliest and most notable intellectual contributions.[147] Nor has the inner doubt vanished to this day. Two referenda on sovereignty have left Quebecers as divided as ever about their status within Canada. Suicide figures for Quebec, especially for young males, remain among the highest in Canada—not exactly a symptom of collective self-confidence. Quebec today may have a more entrepreneurial ring to it than in the past, with francophones finally having come into their own after two centuries of anglophone economic domination. Quebec may be a more pluri-cultural society than before. But beneath the surface, old fears about survival linger on.

English-speaking Canadians, whose links to the British Empire were always as fleeting as that empire itself was to prove, slowly severed their connections with Britain between 1931 and 1982. Only the crown, suitably Canadianized—Elizabeth II, after all, is also Queen of Canada—lingers on as a symbol of the British connection. Canadians remain too divided on the subject of the monarchy to risk opening it up for debate any time soon. If the Australians eventually decide to make a clean break and become a republic, Canadians may follow suit. But not a moment before.

Canadians are fully conscious of their North American destiny. Yet for all the bravado surrounding the passage of the FTA and NAFTA and our supposed ability to compete with the Americans, many Canadians doubt our capacity to resist the American colossus at the door. At the same time, the Conservative Party is actively seeking to reinforce our existing links with the United States, suggesting that divisions on this score are at least as acute within Canada as a whole as are divisions over the sovereignty question within Quebec.

To this can be added other sources of self-doubt. That of aboriginal peoples, whose very survival has by no means been a sure thing and whose position in Canadian society, especially in urban areas, remains almost as marginal as that of gypsies in many parts of Europe. That of successive immigrant groups, who, despite Canada's multicultural policies, have to wonder how well they will be able to reconcile old cultural values with new or fit into the Canadian vertical mosaic, with its two founding groups at the top.

There are so many different tectonic plates at work in Canada that, in the absence of a single founding myth, it makes agreement about fundamentals all the more difficult to achieve. The Canada clause in the failed Charlottetown Accord of 1991–92 was a good illustration of this. By trying to list all the possible attributes of the country, from aboriginal peoples constituting a third order of government, to Quebec's distinct society character, to the existence of official language minorities, to the promotion of cultural and racial diversity, to gender equality, it ended up pleasing almost no one.

An element of self-doubt, of a work in continual progress, never fully achieved, perhaps never achievable at all, has haunted Canadians through almost 150 years of statehood. (I emphasize *statehood*, not *nationhood*.) It has been the source of frequent conflict—provincial and federal, French Canadian and English Canadian, aboriginal and non-aboriginal—and of no small degree of frustration. This frustration is felt especially when Canadians cast an envious glance at the more complete sense of national identity that prevails south of the border.

Americans do not have the same self-doubt that characterizes Canadians. Theirs is a metaphysics of continental expansion and patriotic unity, cemented through civil war and through the emergence of the United States as the dominant power par excellence of the modern world. And it can easily take forms of self-boosterism and proselytism that leave the rest of the world aghast.

Canadians, I have been arguing throughout this essay, would do better culturally and psychologically by comparing themselves *not* with the country with which they share the larger part of a continent, but with the European countries from which most of them originate and with the European Union that has now appeared on the scene.

Earlier parts of the essay have addressed the British and French legacies in particular. These, I remind the reader, are not trivial parts of the Canadian experience, but an essential, even formative element. Our political culture or more correctly cultures bear their stamp in many important ways, ways that earlier generations of political scientists and economists like Siegfried, Innis, or Brebner helped us to understand.

One of my purposes in writing this essay has been to carry the story forward by focusing, in part, on the European Union. This is a new phase in the history of Europe, one that opens the door to a form of political unity across cultural and linguistic lines without precedent in the modern era. The European Union remains a grouping of countries, each with its own distinct identity. The community institutions, for their part, combine confederal-type structures (e.g., the Council of Ministers in which each of the member states is represented) with organs that are somewhat more federal in character: the European Commission, responsible for the day to day operations of the EU, and the European Parliament, elected by direct suffrage in each of the member countries, albeit with a European and not simply national mandate.

Ever since its beginning, the EU has been a work in progress. Its origins go back to the Iron and Steel Community of 1951, grouping France, West Germany, Italy, and the Benelux countries. This community was followed by the Rome Treaty of 1957 that laid the foundations for the European Community proper. Expansion over time was to bring into its ranks Britain, Ireland, Spain, Portugal, Greece, Denmark, Austria, Finland, Sweden, and, as of 2004, many of the countries of central Europe.

Yet almost from day one, the European experiment has been marked by considerable self-doubt. It was by no means obvious that a shared community in iron and steel would efface, in and of itself, the historical enmity between Germany and France that three times in the course of a century had brought the two countries to war. For this to happen, other factors would also have to come into play, for example, the destruction wrought by World War II and the dependence of all the West European countries on American aid through the Marshall Plan in the late 1940s and early 1950s; the Cold War with its division of both Germany and Europe and the pressure for closer co-operation among its non-communist states; economies of scale that made it imperative that the major European economies become more integrated if they were to be able to rival the American colossus, and the emerging poles of competition in the Far East as well.

The history of European construction has been one of development through fits and starts. For every major step forward (e.g., the Rome Treaty of 1957 and the Maastricht Treaty of 1992 that was to lead to the establishment of a common European currency, the Euro, in many of its member states) there have been significant steps backwards as well. For example, de Gaulle's vetoing of British entry into the European Community in January 1963 set expansion back by a good decade. In the same fashion, national resistance to different aspects of European social or agricultural or labour market policies has frequently held up relevant reforms. Nor has the business of devising a European Constitution proven to be a simple task, from the European Convention that drafted the original document, to fractious European summits that finally approved it, to contentious referendums in various member states that still need to ratify it if it is ever to come into effect. There are many different visions of Europe on offer—a federal vs. a nation-state-based one, an Atlanticist vs. a Euro-centric one, a culturally coherent Europe vs. a many-textured one, one faithful to longstanding religious traditions vs. one secular in character.

If I could put things in a nutshell, I would argue that the European Union is built less on a foundation of shared citizenship and a good deal more on a metaphysics of perpetual doubt. Eduardo Lourenço, a Portuguese writer living in France, summarized this well when he wrote, "Europe is above all else a metaphysical continent. This means that it is within its cultural space that metaphysical inquiry has flourished as a form of perplexity that is both accepted and constantly challenged."[148] For anthropologist Constantin von Barloewen, "The specific element of European culture is the capacity to not insist on self-sufficiency and to reject certainty about oneself.... The strength of European culture resides precisely in uncertainty when faced with specific norms, in its capacity for self-criticism."[149]

The cynic might note that Europe has a good deal to be self-critical about. After all, it is the continent of the Inquisition and the Thirty Years War; of the St. Bartholomew massacre and the expulsion of the Huguenots from France; of revolutionary terror and counter-revolutionary blood baths; of gulags, genocide, and ethnic cleansing. Hans Magnus Enzensberger, the German literary critic, talks about "Europeans [taking] shelter behind a collective amnesia ... in the first years after the war."[150] Sudipta Kaviraj speaks of "alienation, ... wars, ... the looming presence of the state which often crosses over from discipline into totalitarianism."[151]

Yet as Ernest Renan argued in *What is a Nation?* (his famous essay of 1882), a crucial feature of national development is the ability to forget.[152] Or more correctly, it is the ability to acknowledge that crimes did indeed occur in the past, but that the collectivity should now attempt to build anew in a different way. In a sense, that is what the attempt at constructing Europe on a consensual basis for all its peoples is about—burying a chequered history of conflict, transcending the bloodshed that has all too often accompanied this conflict in the search for a different kind of future. Canada may have less of a burden to bear in this regard than Europe. Still, there are debts to pay where the treatment of aboriginal peoples has been concerned. Memories of the Conquest have not entirely vanished in Quebec, despite the fact that French Canadians subsequently achieved a full measure of democratic rights and of provincial autonomy for that province. Canada's barring of Oriental immigrants for a long period of time, restrictions against Jews fleeing Europe in the 1930s, or expulsion of Japanese-Canadians from the West Coast during World War II are also not among the country's proudest moments. But like the nations Renan wrote about, or the Europeans today, Canadians, while acknowledging sins of the past, need to get on with charting a different kind of future.

In the case of Europe, that future entails a complex form of citizenship. As William Wallace puts it, "Multi-level government implies multiple loyalties and identities, distributing a degree of legitimacy to each; citizens who define themselves as Bavarians in some contexts, Germans in others, and Europeans in perhaps the broadest political context."[153] European citizenship rests on a series of concentric or nested identities, with the local and the regional levels coexisting side by side with national loyalties and with an element of common European citizenship topping these off. The last is still very much in the realm of a *desideratum* rather than a functioning reality, for there exists no European citizenship in isolation from national ones. Nor do the existence of mobility rights within the EU, of references to the EU on all EU member state passports, or of an elected European Parliament with a serious democratic deficit when compared to national parliaments eclipse the primacy of the nation-state level.

What helps give the EU and its still largely symbolic citizenship a measure of legitimacy is that major European states (e.g., the United Kingdom and France) have had to come to terms with the loss of earlier imperial roles and with their concomitant status as great powers. This loss of status was reinforced in the case of a country like Germany by the experience of the Nazi period and of postwar division into two. In the case of Eastern Europe, forty-five years of Soviet occupation and forced isolation from the West have made membership in the EU a way of rejoining a world that was lost. Within the EU, moreover, no one state can dominate. This situation imposes a spirit, if not of humility, then supportive of the limitations of any one state's power, all the more when it comes to measuring up against the United States.

This sense of limitations is something Canadians can fully comprehend, given a slow severance from imperial ideas on the English Canadian side, a sentiment of long-time subordination to an English-speaking majority on the French Canadian side, and the concentric or nested regional identities that have characterized this country from the very beginning. Furthermore, one of the main attributes of Canadian identity continues to be a sense of the country's subordinate position as a nation-state in its relations with the US.

So the metaphysics of self-doubt unites Canadians with Europeans in a curious sort of way. "[T]he unity of Europe is more a mental construct, the foundation myth of a pluralist civilization, than it is a reality that may be experienced,"[154] writes Hélène Ahrweiler, a distinguished scholar of Byzantine civilization. "If the past fifty years teaches us anything, it is that Europe has a frustrating habit of dashing the hopes of many citizens who keep waiting for a new Europe to arrive ... European unity has shed light on Europe's divisions between the rich states and poor, between the West and the East, between the nationalists and the federalists, and so on," writes William Hitchcock, an American authority on European integration.[155]

Many unanswered questions remain. Will the Europe of the future be a two-track Europe, with a stronger, more integrated core made up of countries like France, Germany, the Benelux states, Italy, and Spain and a looser, more peripheral grouping of countries opposed to further European integration composed of the United Kingdom, Scandinavia, and the Central European states? Will the Europe of the future be one reasonably open to immigration and to the integration of new immigrants or one that is not? Will it be an inward-looking Europe or a cosmopolitan one? A utilitarian Europe driven primarily by economic ideals or one marked by more reflective dimensions of existence that Nietzsche associated with what he called "good Europeans"?[156]

One can pose all kinds of similar questions about the future of Canada—about Canadian unity, about aboriginal identities, about the Canadian experience with official multiculturalism, about our chequered relationship with the United States—with no more certainty, in the end, about where things may be heading than one has about Europe. Canadians are not by disposition a metaphysically-inclined people, nor would they be prone to search for meaning in diverse and enigmatic aspects of existence, in the way that Nietzsche might have asked of his "good Europeans." But in a more down-to-earth sort of way, perhaps they can aspire to becoming "good Canadians" and "good cosmopolitans."

Because they know from the inside the kind of fault-lines—language, culture, identity—that make Canada a splintered, often troubled, federation, Canadians may be better equipped to re-think national identity along multinational lines. Because they have experienced some of the inner doubts and failures that constitute an important part of the modern condition, they may be better able to look at the world in an open-ended way that makes them attuned to other voices. And in doing so, they may find themselves more and more resembling contemporary Europeans, challenged to co-exist on a continent where old atavistic gods may be slowly giving way to something more indeterminate, but more promising.

Let me return to the Canadian identity puzzle one last time. Is Canada best described as a post-modern nation-state with no single overarching national narrative? Is Canada a multi-layered entity, akin to the European Union, experiencing some of the same identity crises the EU encounters as a permanent part of its destiny? Or is Canada simply a more European sort of state in North America? Each of these formulations contains a kernel of truth, though I lean most strongly towards the third.

What began as an offshoot of European colonization has come to resemble, at the start of the twenty-first century, the continent from which the overwhelming majority of its population—of French, British, and of diverse cultural origins—originally derive. Canadians are more European in their reflexes, their behaviour, and ultimately their destiny as citizens of a sovereign North American state than they have been prepared to acknowledge. Perhaps Canada is ultimately a Euro-American state, situated on the doorstep of the most unabashedly American of New World states, a state that would fit remarkably well into the European Union, were it located on the European continent, but which finds itself instead on the North American. And our fate as Canadians may well lie in bridging the divide between the geographical, physical, and economic North Americanness that we share with the United States and the more existential features of our identity that we share with the continent of Europe.

NOTES

CHAPTER TWO

1 H. Blair Neatby, *The Politics of Chaos: Canada in the Thirties*, quoted in Seymour Martin Lipset, *Continental Divide: The values and institutions of the United States and Canada* (New York and London: Routledge, 1990), p. 54.

2 Quoted in Jim Garrison, *America as Empire* (San Francisco: Berrett-Koehler, 2004), pp. 61–62 and in Robert Kagan, *Of Paradise and Power* (New York: Knopf, 2003), p. 88.

3 Walt Whitman, "Thou Mother with Thy Equal Brood," *The Complete Poetry and Selected Prose of Walt Whitman*, ed. James E. Miller, Jr. (Boston: Houghton Mifflin, 1959), p. 318.

4 Jules Michelet, *Introduction à l'histoire universelle*, quoted in Tzvetan Todorov, *Nous et les Autres* (Paris: Seuil, 1989), p. 241.

5 Quoted in François Azouvi, *Descartes et la France* (Paris: Fayard, 2002), p. 316.

6 Hannah Arendt, *On Revolution* (New York: Viking Press, 1965).

7 John Schwarzmantel, *Citizenship and Identity* (London: Routledge, 2003), p. 75.

8 "Les nations ne jettent pas à l'écart leurs antiques moeurs, comme on se dépouille d'un vieil habit. On leur en peut arracher quelques parties, mais il en reste des lambeaux qui forment, avec les nouveaux vêtements, un effroyable bigarrure." Chateaubriand, *Le Génie du Christianisme*, 3ème partie, livre 1, chap. 8.

9 Anthony D. Smith, *Nationalism: Theory, Ideology, History* (Cambridge: Polity Press, 2001), p. 13.

10 Charles Mair, *Tecumseh, a drama and Canadian poems* (Toronto: The Radisson Society of Canada, 1926), p. 143.

11 Quoted in Desmond Morton, "Divided Loyalties? Divided Country?" in *Belonging: The Meaning of Canadian Citizenship*, ed. William Kaplan (Montreal: McGill-Queen's University Press, 1993), p. 56.

12 John Seeley, *The Expansion of England* (1883), quoted in Norman Davies, *The Isles: A History* (Oxford: Oxford University Press, 1999), p. 867.

13 Quoted in Carl Berger, *The Sense of Power: Studies in the Ideas of Canadian Imperialism, 1867–1914* (Toronto: University of Toronto Press, 1970), p. 80.

14 Quoted in Robert Fulford, "A Post-Modern Dominion," in *Belonging*, ed. William Kaplan, p. 110.

15 Quoted in Berger, *The Sense of Power*, p. 231.

16 Hector Fabre, "La société française au Canada," in *Le rouge et le bleu: Une anthologie de la pensée politique au Québec de la Conquête à la Révolution tranquille*, ed. Yvan Lamonde and Claude Corbo (Montréal: Presses de l'Université de Montréal, 1999), pp. 272–74.

17 Quoted in André Siegfried, *The Race Question in Canada*, ed. Frank H. Underhill, Carleton Library Series, no. 29 (1906; reprint, Ottawa: Carleton University Press, 1966), pp. 91–92.

18 Olivar Asselin, *Pourquoi on aime la France* (Paris: Imp. de Vaugirard, 1916) in *Le rouge et le bleu*, p. 343.

19 Quoted in Siegfried, *The Race Question*, p. 174.

20 Ibid., p. 175.

21 Henri Bourassa, "Race et civilisation française," cited in Sylvie Lacombe, *La rencontre de deux peuples élus* (Sainte-Foy: Presses de l'Université Laval, 2002), pp. 39, 46, 51.

22 Quoted in John Meisel, Guy Rocher, Arthur Silver, eds., *As I Recall/ Si je me souviens* (Montreal: Institute for Research on Public Policy, 1999), p. 98.

23 Sylvie Lacombe provides an excellent account of this dialogue of the deaf in her book, *La rencontre de deux peuples élus* (Sainte-Foy: Les Presses de l'Université Laval, 2002).

CHAPTER THREE

24 John Brebner, *North Atlantic Triangle*, Carleton Library Series 30 (1945; Ottawa: Carleton University Press, 1966), p. 325.

25 Michel Brunet *Canadians et Canadiens* (Montréal, 1952), cited in *As I Recall*, op. cit., p. 35.

26 Margaret Thatcher, "The European Family of Nations," Bruges speech, Sept. 1988, in *The Eurosceptical Reader*, ed. Martin Holmes (Basingstoke: Palgrave Macmillan, 1996), p. 91.

27 European Commission, *How Europeans see themselves: Looking through the mirror with public opinion surveys* (Brussels: European Commission, 2001), p. 11.

28 "From Confederacy to Federation—Thoughts on the finality of European integration," Speech by Joschka Fischer at the Humboldt University in Berlin, 12 May 2000, http://www.auswaertigesamt.de/www/en/eu_politik/ausgabe_archiv? suche=1&archiv_id=1027&bereich_id=4&type_id=3 (accessed January 1, 2005).

29 European Commission, *How Europeans see themselves*, pp. 10–11.

30 Cited in Sonja P. Reikmann, "The Myth of European Unity in Myths and Nationhood," *Myths and Nationhood*, ed. Geoffrey Hoskins and George Schopflin (London: Hurst, 1997), pp. 65–66.

31 André Malraux, *Conférence en Sorbonne*, 1946 in Yvan Hersant and Fabienne Durand-Bogaert, eds., *Europe* (Paris: Robert Laffont, 2000), p. 934.

32 Karl Jaspers, Conference, Sept. 13, 1946, in Hersant and Durand-Bogaert, eds., *Europes*, p. 472.

33 J.H.H. Weiler, "Does Europe Need a Constitution?" in Peter Gowan and Perry Anderson, eds., *The Question of Europe* (London: Verso, 1997), p. 288.

34 The Dominion Institute, History Teachers Survey, 2001, http://www.dominion. ca/English/polls.html (accessed January 1, 2005).

CHAPTER FOUR

35 Cf. the articles by Denis Delage, Jocelyn Létourneau, Jane Jensen and Danielle Juteau in *Vive Quebec!: new thinking and new approaches to the Quebec nation*, ed. Michel Venne (Toronto: James Lorimer, 2001).

36 Cf. the articles by Jacques Beauchemin and Serge Cantin in *Vive Quebec!: new thinking and new approaches to the Quebec nation*, ed. Michel Venne (Toronto: James Lorimer, 2001).

37 Jocelyn Maclure, *Quebec Identity: The Challenge of Pluralism* (Montreal: McGill-Queen's University Press, 2003), p. 141.

38 Catalonian Cultural Committee, *Appeal on Behalf of Catalonia* (Geneva, 1927) quoted in Joshua Fishman, "Language and Nationalism," in *Nationalism in Europe 1815 to the present: A reader*, ed. Stuart Woolf (London: Routledge, 1996), p. 160.

39 See Maurice Pinard, Robert Bernier, and Vincent Lemieux, *Un combat inachevé* (Sainte-Foy: Les Presses de l'Université du Québec, 1997), p. 320, table 10.

40 Friedrich Hölderlin, "Im Walde," quoted in Dennis I. Schmidt, *On Germans and Other Greeks: Tragedy and Ethical Life* (Bloomington: Indiana University Press, 2001), p. 149.

41 Martin Heidegger, "Letter on Humanism," *Basic Writings* (New York: Harper and Row, 1977), p. 193.

42 Bernard Meltzer and Gil Richard Musolf, "Resentment and Ressentiment," *Sociological Inquiry* 72, no. 2 (2002): 251.

43 Patrick Vankrunkelsven, Co-President, Intergovernmental and Inter-parliamentary Conference on Constitutional Renewal, interviewed by Sophie Perrier, *Libération* 11 November 1999.

44 Cf. Bernard Crick, "The English and the British," in *National Identities: The Constitution of the United Kingdom*, ed. Bernard Crick (Oxford: Blackwell, 1991), pp. 90-104. Simon Heffer, *Nor Shall My Sword: The Reinvention of England* (London: Weidenfeld & Nicolson, 1999), p. 10.

45 Keith Robbins, "The United Kingdom as a Multi-national State," in *Nationalism in Europe: Past and Present*, ed. J. Beramendi, R. Maiz, and X. Nunez (Universidad de Santiago de Compostela, 1994), 2: 315.

46 Leger and Leger Poll of Oct. 23–6, 1995, "Self-Identification of Quebec Francophones," in Kenneth McRoberts, *Misconceiving Canada: The Struggle for National Unity* (Toronto: Oxford University Press, 1997), p. 247.

47 See Michael Keating, *Nations against the State: The New Politics of Nationalism in Quebec, Catalonia and Scotland* (Basingstoke: Macmillan, 1996), p. 132, table 5.2.

48 A 1995 survey by the Rowntree Trust, cited by Richard Weight, *Patriots: National Identities in Britain, 1940–2000* (Basingstoke: Macmillan, 2002), p. 696.

49 John Stuart Mill, "Of Nationality, as Connected with Representative Government," bk. 16 of *Representative Government* (1861; reprint, London: Dent, 1968), p. 361.

50 Quoted by Sven Papcke, "Who Needs European Identity?" in *The Idea of Europe: Problems of National and Transnational Identity*, ed. Brian Nelson, David Roberts, and Walter Veit (New York/Oxford: Berg, 1992), p. 70.

51 Soledad Garcia, ed., *European Identity and the Search for Legitimacy* (London: St Martin's Press, 1993), p. 13.

52 Umberto Eco, quoted in *Le Monde*, 18-19 April 2004, p. 6.

53 Helmut Kohl, quoted in "EU newcomers welcomed to the club," *BBC News*, 1 May 2004, http://news.bbc.co.uk/go/pr/fr/-/1/hi/world/europe/3675801.stm (accessed January 1, 2005).

CHAPTER FIVE

54 Canada. Royal Commission on Dominion-Provincial Relations, *The Growth of Government Activities since Confederation*, study prepared for the Royal Commission on Dominion-Provincial Relations, by John A. Corry (Ottawa: Government Printing Office, 1939).

55 Tom Kent, "Mike Pearson was most at home with Scandinavian governments," interview by Michael Enright, *The Sunday Edition*, CBC Radio, 4 April 2004.

56 Jean Lesage, 3 June 1961, quoted in Réjean Pelletier, "Les partis politiques et l'État," in *L'etat du Québec en devenir*, ed. Gérard Bergeron and Réjean Pelletier (Montréal: Boréal, 1980), p. 245.

57 Pauline Maurois, *Le Devoir*, 20 April 2004.

58 Will Hutton, *The World We're In* (London: Little Brown, 2002), p. 16.

59 Kenneth Dyson, *The State Tradition in Western Europe* (Oxford: Martin Robertson, 1980), p. 272.

60 "Il n'est pas bon d'être trop libre." Blaise Pascal, *Pensées*, no. 90 (Paris: Le Livre de Poche, 2000), p. 79.

61 Judith and Andrew Kleinfeld, "Cowboy Nation and American Character," *Society* (March-April 2004): 43–50, 46.

62 See the article by Brian Michael and Michael Wolfson, "Income inequality in North America: Does the 49th Parallel Still Matter?" *The Canadian Economic Observer*, August 2000, cited in Michael Adams, *Fire and Ice: The United States, Canada and the Myth of Converging Values* (Toronto: Penguin, 2003), p. 62.

63 Clifford Krauss, "Canada's View on Social Issues is Opening Rifts with the United States," *New York Times*, 2 December 2003.

64 UNESCO, *World Culture Report 2000*, p. 229, table 10.

65 Michael Adams, *Sex in the Snow* (Toronto: Viking, 1997), p. 171.

66 Andrew Vincent, *Nationalism and Particularity* (Cambridge: Cambridge University Press, 2002), p. 108.

67 "[B]orderless systems often overestimate their moral and legitimate power.... The social welfare state ... can be realized only 'within borders.' This implies a mode of socialization limited to the nation-state." Claus Offe, "The Democratic Welfare State in an Integrating Europe," in *Democracy Beyond the State?*, ed. Michael Greven and Louis Pauly (Lanham, MD: Rowman and Littlefield, 2000), p. 85.

68 T.H. Marshall, *Citizenship and Social Class and Other Essays* (Cambridge: Cambridge University Press, 1950).

69 Gary Gardner, Erik Assadourian, and Radhika Sarin, "The State of Consumption Today," in *State of the World 2004*, ed. Brian Halwell and Lisa Mastey (New York: W.W. Norton, 2004), p. 17. The authors estimate that, at the global level, an ecological footprint of 1.9 hectares of biologically productive land per person represents a sustainable level of resource expenditure.

70 Quoted by Kevin Phillips, *Boiling Point* (New York: Random House, 1993), p. 167.

CHAPTER SIX

71 There is a good discussion of the origins of Canada's multicultural policy in Kenneth McRoberts, *Misconceiving Canada: The Struggle for National Unity* (Toronto: Oxford University Press, 1997), chapter 5.

72 A number of the intervenors at the hearings of the Spicer Commission, set up in the aftermath of the failure of the Meech Lake Accord, made comments along these lines. See "No More Hyphenated Canadians," Citizens' Forum on Canada's Future, *Report to the People of Canada* (Ottawa: Supply and Services Canada, 1991), pp. 88–89.

73 "Or, particulièrement à Montréal, le multiculturalisme est insidieux, car il rend légitime et psychologiquement incontournable le bilinguisme institutionnel." Bruno Roy, Président, Comité langue et souveraineté. Union des écrivaines et des écrivains québécois, "Montréal, ville internationale de langue française—La

future Charte montréalaise des droits et responsabilités doit protéger la langue de la majorité française," *Le Devoir*, 4 May 2004.

74 UNESCO, *World Culture Report 2000*, p. 238, table 20.

75 This notion was advanced by Will Kymlicka at the conference *Citoyenneté 2020—S'engager pour notre avenir* in Montreal, 20–21 October 2000.

76 The Right Honourable Beverley McLachlin, Chief Justice of Canada, "The Civilization of Difference," Fourth Annual LaFontaine-Baldwin Lecture, Halifax, 7 March 2003.

77 "Pride in National Achievements," in UNESCO *World Culture Report 2000*, p. 230, table 11.

78 Jonathan Sacks, Chief Rabbi of Britain, "[W]e each have to be bilingual. There is a first and public language of citizenship which we have to learn if we are to live together. And there is a variety of second languages which connect us to our local framework of relationships: to family and group and the traditions that underlie them. If we are to achieve integration without assimilation, it is important to give each of these languages its due." *The Persistence of Faith* (London: Weidenfeld and Nicolson, 1991), quoted in David Miller, *On Nationality* (Oxford: Oxford University Press, 1995), p. 138.

79 My thinking in these matters is fairly close to what Maurizio Viroli argues in his defence of a republican form of patriotism, *For Love of Country: An Essay on Patriotism and Nationalism* (Oxford: Clarendon, 1995).

CHAPTER SEVEN

80 Robert Kagan, *Of Paradise and Power* (New York: Knopf, 2003), p. 87.

81 Herman Melville, *White Jacket* (New York, 1850), chap. 36, quoted in Andrew Bacevich, *American Empire* (Cambridge, MA: Harvard University Press, 2002), p. 43.

82 Quoted in William Pfaff, "The American Mission?", review of *The Choice: Global Domination or Global Leadership*, by Zbigniew Brzezinski, *The New York Review of Books*, 51, no. 6 (2004): 28.

83 Quoted in Michael Hardt and Antonio Negri, "Empire," *Transform! European Network for Alternative Thinking and Political Dialog*, http://www.transform-network.de/index.phpp (accessed October 5, 2004).

84 Hugh Innis, ed., *Americanization* (Toronto: McGraw-Hill Ryerson, 1972), p. 1.

85 James C. Bennett, "An Anglosphere Primer," Online document presented to the Foreign Policy Research Institute, 2001, http://www.pattern.com/bennettj-anglosphereprimer.html (accessed January 1, 2005).

86 The Honorable Richard B. Cheney, "Meeting the Challenge of the War on Terrorism," Heritage Lecture #802, October 17, 2003, http://www.heritage.org/Research/MiddleEast/HL802.cfm (accessed January 1, 2005).

87 The Honorable George W. Bush, "Turning Back the Terrorist Threat: America's Unbreakable Commitment," Heritage Lecture #809 November 19, 2003, http://www.heritage.org/Research/MiddleEast/HL809.cfm (accessed January 1, 2005).

88 An Ekos Research poll for the newspapers *La Presse* and the *Toronto Star* on March 21, 2003, showed that 71 per cent of Canadians supported their government's decision not to send troops to Iraq in the absence of a resolution from the UN Security Council authorizing such action. A CRIC Press Release, April 9, 2003, "Canadians Differ from Americans on Iraq, United Nations," highlights an Environics poll in March 2003, showing that 80 per cent of Canadian respondents see the United Nations contributing a great deal to world peace versus 59 per cent of American respondents answering YES to a similar question, and 66 per cent of Canadians favouring the peaceful disarmament of Iraq versus 46 per cent of American respondents. http://www.cric.ca/en_html/publications/sondages_cric.html (accessed January 1, 2005).

89 An IPSOS Reid poll, on April 6, 2003, showed equal numbers of Canadians supporting (48 per cent) and opposing (48 per cent) the US led military action against Iraq, with a majority (54 per cent) in English Canada now supporting the war, and only 29 per cent in Quebec doing so.

90 Robert Kagan, *Of Paradise and Power: America and Europe in the New World Order* (New York: Alfred A. Knopf, 2003), p. 99.

91 George Orwell, "Gandhi in Mayfair," *Horizon*, September 1943, quoted in Gordon Bowker, *George Orwell* (London: Little Brown, 2003), p. 367.

92 Jeffrey Simpson, "They're Mars, We're Venus," *Globe and Mail*, 21 March 2003, A17.

93 UNESCO, *World Culture Report 2000*, p. 229, table 10.

94 Kagan, *Of Paradise and Power*, p. 55.

95 Carl Bild, quoted by Thomas Friedman, "The End of the West," *New York Times*, 2 November 2003.

96 Quoted by Thomas Friedman, *The Lexus and the Olive Tree* (New York. Anchor edition, 2000), p. 384.

97 "Pit-Stop Presidency," *Washington Post*, 27 October 2002, B7, quoted in Ivo H. Daalder and James. M. Lindsay, *America Unbound: The Bush Revolution in Foreign Policy* (Washington: Brookings Institute, 2003), p. 195.

98 *New York Times Book Review*, 22 June 2003, p. 9, quoted in Daalder and Lindsay, *America Unbound*, p. 189.

99 Official in Milan, 1570, quoted in Henry Kamen, *Spain's Road to Empire* (London: Allen Lane, 2002), p. 509.

100 Quoted by Friedman, *The Lexus and the Olive Tree*, p. 384.

101 Fareed Zakaria, "The Arrogant Empire," *Newsweek*, 24 March 2003, cited in Daalder and Lindsay, *America Unbound*, p. 190.

102 Adam Pulchart, quoted in *International Herald Tribune*, 4 March 2004, http://www.iht.com/articles/508769.html (accessed January 1, 2005).

103 "Majorities in the three countries—historically Washington's closest NATO partners—also said that as a consequence of the war they had less confidence that the United States is trustworthy. Mistrust was expressed by 82 percent in Germany, 78 percent in France and 58 percent in Britain. According to François Heisbourg, director of the Foundation for Strategic Research in Paris, alienation is increasing in Europe 'because there's been no give on the Bush side. There is a widespread perception in Europe that we have the choice of being treated as a vassal—a poodle in the case of Britain—or being treated as an antagonist,' Heisbourg said." Meg Bortin, "European distrust of U.S. role sharpens," *International Herald Tribune*, 17 March 2004, http://www.iht.com/ articles/510613.htm (accessed January 1, 2005).

104 "74 per cent of respondents [to a *Globe and Mail*-CTV News poll] said that the federal government made the correct decision by not joining the US-led coalition that invaded Iraq." Jeff Sallot, "Bush lied to justify Iraq war, Canada right to stay out: poll," *Globe and Mail*, 15 March 2004.

105 Claude Julien, *Le Canada: Dernière Chance de l'Europe* (Paris: Grasset, 1968).

106 William Pfaff, *The Wrath of Nations* (New York: Simon and Schuster, 1993), p. 25.

107 Hanspeter Neuhold, "Transatlantic Turbulence: Rift or Ripples," *European Foreign Affairs Review* 8 (2003): 467.

108 Peter Schneider, "Separated by civilization: Trans-Atlantic impasse," *International Herald Tribune*, 7 April 2004, http://www.iht.com/articles/ 513613.html (accessed January 1, 2005).

CHAPTER EIGHT

109 Jean de Crèvecoeur, *Letters from an American Farmer* (London: Printed for T. Davies, 1782), in *The American Spirit: U.S. History as Seen by Contemporaries*, ed. Thomas A. Bailey (Boston: Heath, 1968), p. 68.

110 Cf. Jane Errington, *The Lion, the Eagle, and Upper Canada* (Montreal: McGill-Queen's University Press, 1994); S.J.R. Noel, *Patrons, Clients, Brokers: Ontario Society and Politics, 1791-1896* (Toronto: University of Toronto Press, 1990), p. 31; and Edward Grabb, James Curtis, Douglas Baer, "Defining Moments and Recurring Myths: Comparing Canadians and Americans after the American Revolution," *Canadian Review of Sociology and Anthropology* 37, no.4 (2000): 373-419.

111 Alexis de Tocqueville, *Democracy in America*, trans. Henry Reeve, 2 volumes (New York: Schocken Books, 1961), vol. 1, p. 517, originally quoted in Grabb, Curtis and Baer, "Defining Moments," p. 383.

112 Quoted in Grabb, Curtis, and Baer, "Defining Moments," p. 383.

113 de Tocqueville, *Democracy in America*, vol.1, p. 516.

114 Joseph Yvon Thériault, *Critique de l'américanité: Mémoire et démocratie au Québec* (Montréal: Québec-Amérique, 2002), p. 32.

115 Jean Morisset, "A propos de la série 'L'américanité': promenade dans une Amérique en quête du Québec," *Séquences*, 135–136 (September 1988): 38–43, quoted in Thériault, *Critique de l'américanité*, pp. 32–33.

116 Joseph Levitt, *Henri Bourassa and the golden calf; the social program of the Nationalists of Quebec (1900-1914)* (Ottawa: Les Editions de l'Université d'Ottawa, 1972).

117 André Laurendeau, *Le Devoir*, 8 March 1961, quoted in James Bickerton, Stephen Brooks, and Alain-G. Gagnon, *Six penseurs en quête de liberté, d'égalité et de communauté* (Sainte-Foy: Les Presses de l'Universite Laval, 2003), pp. 71–72.

118 Thériault, *Critique de l'américanité*, p. 117.

119 Anne Legaré, *Le Québec otage de ses alliés: Les relations du Québec avec la France et les États-Unis* (Montréal: VLB Éditeur, 2003), pp. 250–51 and 271.

120 Chris Patten, "Who Do They Think We Are? Being British," *The Political Quarterly*, 73, no. 2 (April-June 2002): 131.

121 Quoted in Cris Shore and Annabel Black, "Citizens' Europe and the Construction of European Identity," in *The Anthropology of Europe* ed. Victoria A. Goddard, Joseph Llobera, and Cris Shore (Oxford: Berg, 1994), p. 288.

122 Göran Therborn, "The World's Trader, the World's Lawyer. Europe and Global Resources," *European Journal of Social Theory*, Vol. 5, no. 4 (November 2002): 415.

123 Denis de Rougemont, *Vingt-huit siècles d'Europe*, cited in Max Gallo, "Europe without Nations: An Artifice, a Dangerous Mirage," in *Cultural Politics and Political Culture in Postmodern Europe*, ed. Peter Burgess (Amsterdam: Rodopi, 1997), p. 382.

124 See Fernando Pessoa's manifesto for the journal *Orpheu*, published in 1915: "Europe rather than America is the source and origin of this type of [cosmopolitan] civilization which serves as norm and orientation to the entire world." Cited in Timothy Brennan, "Cosmopolitanism and Internationalism," in *Debating Cosmopolitics*, ed. Daniele Archibugi (London: Verso, 2003), p. 45.

125 See Ernst Bloch's impressive three volume work, *The Principle of Hope* (Oxford: Basil Blackwell, 1986), for one evocation of the utopian tradition.

126 Agnes Heller, "Europe: An Epilogue?" in *The Idea of Europe: Problems of National and Transnational identity*, ed. Brian Nelson, David Roberts, and Walter Veit (New York and Oxford: Berg, 1992), p. 25.

127 Michael Th. Greven, "Can the European Union Finally Become a Democracy?" in *Democracy Beyond the State?* ed. Michael Th. Greven and Louis Pauly (Lanham: Rowman & Littlefield, 2000), p. 53.

128 "Europe is a small continent with a long history of self-awareness, which means that to be a European is to have an identity rather more precise than that attaching to persons who are 'African' or 'Asian' or 'American' by virtue of their geographical origin." Tony Judt, *A Grand Illusion? An Essay on Europe* (New York: Hill and Wang, 1996), p. 45.

129 European Convention. Secretariat, *Draft Treaty Establishing a Constitution for Europe*, treaty adopted by consensus by the European Convention on 13 June and 10 July 2003 and submitted to the President of the European Council in Rome, 18 July 2003, http://european-convention.eu.int/docs/Treaty/cv00850.en03.pdf (accessed January 2, 2005).

130 Pat Cox, "Let's have a genuine Euro debate," BBC website, June 1, 2004, http://news.bbc.co.uk/1/hi/world/europe/3750207.stm (accessed January 2, 2005).

CHAPTER NINE

131 Harold Innis, "The Strategy of Culture," quoted in Donald Creighton, *Harold Adams Innis, Portrait of a Scholar* (Toronto: University of Toronto Press, 1957), p. 143.

132 Michael Adams, *Fire and Ice*, "North America's Two Distinct Societies," chapter 2.

133 Seymour Martin Lipset, *Continental Divide*, p. 88.

134 Neil MacKinnon and Alison Luke, "Changes in Identity Attitudes as Reflections of Social and Cultural Change," *Canadian Journal of Sociology*, 27, no. 3 (2002): 318.

135 Julian Young, *The Death of God and the Meaning of Life* (London: Routledge, 2003).

136 Stephen Bates, "Still one nation under God," *The Guardian*, 21 December 2002.

137 Quoted by Sidney Blumenthal, "The Religious Warrior of Abu Ghraib," *The Guardian*, 20 May 2004.

138 John Sutherland, "God Save America," *The Guardian*, 4 May 2004. The 59 per cent figure cited comes from a *Time* magazine poll.

139 "What distinguishes us from our southern neighbours is the Christian right—here, they make up 10 per cent of the population; in the United States, the number is at least triple that much." Neil Nevitte, quoted in Doug Saunders, "So, our Conservatives aren't progressive any more," *Globe and Mail*, 22 May 2004.

140 Quoted by William Pfaff, "A new American dream," *The Observer*, 16 May 2004.

141 Antonio Muñoz Molina, Spanish writer, "El artista consentido," *El Pais*, 17 April 2004.

142 André Laurendeau, "The Conditions for the Existence of a National Culture," in *Canadian Political Thought*, ed. H.D. Forbes (Toronto: Oxford University Press), p. 275.

143 Marcel Rioux, *Un peuple dans le siècle* (Montréal: Boréal, 1990), p. 254.

144 Slavoj Zizek, "What Does Europe Want?" *In These Times*, 1 May 2004.

145 *Le Monde*, Editorial, 14 May 2004.

CHAPTER TEN

146 For an excellent account of the role that melancholy can play in the nationalist discourse of smaller peoples, see the account of Basque nationalism in Jon Juaristi, *El Bucle Melancólico: Historias de Nacionalistas Vascos* (Madrid: Espasa Hoy, 1997). See also Jocelyn Maclure, *Quebec Identity: The Challenge of Pluralism* (Montréal: McGill-Queen's University Press, 2003), chapter 1.

147 István Bibó, "The Distress of East European Small States," especially section 4 on the deformation of political culture, in István Bibó, *Democracy, revolution, self-determination: selected writings*, ed. Károly Nagy, Social Science Monographs, (Highland Lakes: Atlantic Research Publications; New York: Distributed by Columbia University Press, 1991); Pierre Trudeau, "Quebec on the Eve of the Asbestos Strike," in *The Asbestos Strike*, ed. Pierre Elliott Trudeau (Toronto: James Lewis & Samuel, 1974).

148 Eduardo Lourenço, "De l'Europe comme culture," reprinted in *Europes*, ed. Yves Hersant and Fabienne Durand-Bogaert (Paris: Robert Laffont, Bouquins, 2000), p. 788.

149 Constantin von Barloewen, *Anthropologie de la mondialisation* (Paris: Edition des Syrtes, 2003), p. 241.

150 Hans Magnus Enzensberger quoted by Tony Judt, *A Grand Illusion*, p. 83.

151 Sudipta Kaviraj, Univ. of London, "Literature and the Moral Imagination of Modernity," in *The Moral Fabric in Contemporary Societies*, ed. Grazyna Skapska and Annamaria Orla-Bukowska (Leiden: Brill, 2003), p. 278.

152 "The essence of a nation is that all individuals have many things in common and have also forgotten many things.... Every French citizen has forgotten Saint-Bartholomew and the massacres in Midi in the 13th century." Ernest Renan, *Qu'est ce qu'une nation?* (Paris: Agora, 1992), p. 42.

153 William Wallace, "Rescue or Retreat? The Nation State in Western Europe, 1945–93," in *The Question of Europe*, ed. Peter Gowan and Perry Anderson (London: Verso, 1997), p. 44.

154 Hélène Ahrweiler, "Roots and Trends in European Culture," in *The Idea of Europe*, ed. Brian Nelson, David Roberts, and Walter Veit (London: Berg, 1992), p. 31.

155 William Hitchcock, *The Struggle for Europe* (New York: Doubleday, 2003), pp. 458–59.

156 Nietzsche's use of the phrase "good European" is scattered through a number of his works, including *The Gay Science* and *Beyond Good and Evil*. Stefan Elbe offers a compelling reading of the enigmatic and reflective elements one can associate with this term in his book *Europe: A Nietzschean Perspective* (London: Routledge, 2003), especially chapter 5, "We good Europeans."

BIBLIOGRAPHY

Adams, Michael. *Fire and Ice: The United States, Canada and the Myth of Converging Values.* Toronto: Penguin, 2003.

Adams, Michael. *Sex in the Snow.* Toronto: Viking, 1997.

Ahrweiler, Hélène. "Roots and Trends in European Culture." In *The Idea of Europe,* ed. Brian Nelson, David Roberts, and Walter Vei. London: Berg, 1992.

Archibugi, Daniele, ed. *Debating Cosmopolitics.* London: Verso, 2003.

Arendt, Hannah. *On Revolution.* New York: Viking Press, 1965.

Azouvi, François. *Descartes et la France.* Paris: Fayard, 2002.

Bacevich, Andrew. *American Empire.* Cambridge, MA: Harvard University Press, 2002.

Barloewen, Constantin von. *Anthropologie de la mondialisation.* Paris: Edition des Syrtes, 2003.

Bates, Stephen. "Still one nation under God." *The Guardian,* 21 December 2002.

Bennett, James C. "An Anglosphere Primer." Online document presented to the Foreign Policy Research Institute, 2001. Available online from http://www.pattern.com/bennettj-anglosphereprimer.html.

Berger, Carl. *The Sense of Power: Studies in the Ideas of Canadian Imperialism, 1867-1914.* Toronto: University of Toronto Press, 1970.

Bergeron, Gérard and Réjean Pelletier, eds. *L'etat du Québec en devenir.* Montréal: Boréal, 1980.

Bibó, István. *Democracy, revolution, self-determination: selected writings.* Ed. Károly Nagy. Social Science Monographs, Highland Lakes: Atlantic Research Publications, 1991; distributed by Columbia University Press.

Bickerton, James, Stephen Brooks, and Alain-G. Gagnon. *Six penseurs en quête de liberté, d'égalité et de communauté.* Sainte-Foy: Les Presses de l'Universite Laval, 2003.

Bloch, Ernst. *The Principle of Hope.* Oxford: Basil Blackwell, 1986.

Blumenthal, Sidney. "The Religious Warrior of Abu Ghraib." *The Guardian,* 20 May 2004.

Bortin, Meg. "European distrust of U.S. role sharpens." *International Herald Tribune,* 17 March 2004.

Bowker, Gordon. *George Orwell.* London: Little Brown, 2003.

Brebner, John. *North Atlantic Triangle.* 1945. Reprint, Carleton Library Series, no. 30. Ottawa: Carleton University Press, 1966.

Brunet, Michel. *Canadians et Canadiens: sur l'histoire de la pensée des deux Canadas.* Montréal: Fides, 1954.

Bush, George W. "Turning Back the Terrorist Threat: America's Unbreakable Commitment." Heritage Lecture Number 809, Heritage Foundation, Washington, DC, 19 November 2003.

Chateaubriand, François-René, vicomte de. *Génie du Christianisme.* Paris: Le Normant, 1823.

Cheney, Richard B. "Meeting the Challenge of the War on Terrorism." Heritage Lecture Number 802, Heritage Foundation, Washington, DC, 17 October 2003.

Citizens' Forum on Canada's Future. *Report to the People of Canada.* Ottawa: Supply and Services Canada, 1991.

Corry, John A. *The Growth of Government Activities since Confederation.* Study prepared for the Royal Commission on Dominion-Provincial Relations. Ottawa: Government Printing Office, 1939.

Cox, Pat. "Let's have a genuine Euro debate." *BBC Website,* 1 June 2004. Available online from http://news.bbc.co.uk/1/hi/world/europe/3750207.stm.

Creighton, Donald. *Harold Adams Innis, Portrait of a Scholar.* Toronto: University of Toronto Press, 1957.

Crèvecoeur, Jean de. *Letters from an American Farmer.* 1782. Reprinted in *The American Spirit: U.S. History as Seen by Contemporaries,* ed. Thomas A. Bailey. Boston: Heath, 1968.

Crick, Bernard. "The English and the British." In *National Identities: The Constitution of the United Kingdom,* ed. Bernard Crick. Oxford: Blackwell, 1991.

Daalder, Ivo H. and James M. Lindsay. *America Unbound: The Bush Revolution in Foreign Policy.* Washington: Brookings Institute, 2003.

Davies, Norman. *The Isles: A History.* Oxford: Oxford University Press, 1999.

The Dominion Institute. *History Teachers Survey,* 2001. Available online from http://www.dominion.ca/English/polls.html.

Dyson, Kenneth. *The State Tradition in Western Europe.* Oxford: Martin Robertson, 1980.

Elbe, Stefan. *Europe: A Nietzschean Perspective.* London: Routledge, 2003.

Errington, Jane. *The Lion, the Eagle, and Upper Canada.* Montreal: McGill-Queen's University Press, 1994.

European Commission. *How Europeans see themselves: Looking through the mirror with public opinion surveys.* Brussels: European Commission, 2001.

European Convention. Secretariat. *Draft Treaty Establishing a Constitution for Europe,* 18 July 2003. Available online from http://european-convention.eu.int/docs/Treaty/cv00850.en03.pdf.

Fischer, Joschka, "From Confederacy to Federation—Thoughts on the finality of European integration," Speech at the Humboldt University in Berlin, 12 May 2000, http://www.auswaertigesamt.de/www/en/eu_politik/ausgabe_archiv?suche=1& archiv_id=1027&bereich_id=4& type_id=3.

Fishman, Joshua. "Language and Nationalism." In *Nationalism in Europe 1815 to the present: A reader*, ed. Stuart Woolf. London: Routledge, 1996.

Forbes, H.D., ed. *Canadian Political Thought*. Toronto: Oxford University Press, 1985.

Friedman, Thomas. *The Lexus and the Olive Tree*. New York: Anchor, 2000.

Garcia, Soledad, ed. *European Identity and the Search for Legitimacy*. London: St Martin's Press, 1993.

Gardner, Gary, Erik Assadourian, and Radhika Sarin, "The State of Consumption Today." In *State of the World 2004*, ed. Brian Halwell and Lisa Mastey. New York: W.W. Norton, 2004.

Garrison, Jim. *America as Empire*. San Francisco: Berrett-Koehler, 2004.

Grabb, Edward, James Curtis, and Douglas Baer "Defining Moments and Recurring Myths: Comparing Canadians and Americans after the American Revolution." *Canadian Review of Sociology and Anthropology* 37, no. 4 (2000): 373-419.

Greven, Michael Th. "Can the European Union Finally Become a Democracy?" In *Democracy Beyond the State?*, ed. Michael Th. Greven

and Louis Pauly. Lanham: Rowman & Littlefield, 2000.

Hardt, Michael and Antonio Negri. "Empire." *Transform! European Network for Alternative Thinking and Political Dialog*. Available online from http://www.transform-network.de/index.phpp.

Heffer, Simon. *Nor Shall My Sword: The Reinvention of England*. London: Weidenfeld & Nicolson, 1999.

Heidegger, Martin. "Letter on Humanism." *Basic Writings*. New York: Harper and Row, 1977.

Heller, Agnes. "Europe: An Epilogue?" In *The Idea of Europe: Problems of National and Transnational identity*, ed. Brian Nelson, David Roberts, and Walter Veit. New York and Oxford: Berg, 1992.

Hersant, Yvan and Fabienne Durand-Bogaert, eds. *Europe*. Paris: Robert Laffont, 2000.

Hitchcock, William. *The Struggle for Europe*. New York: Doubleday, 2003.

Hutton, Will. *The World We're In*. London: Little Brown, 2002.

Innis, Hugh, ed. *Americanization*. Toronto: McGraw-Hill Ryerson, 1972.

Juaristi, Jon. *El Bucle Melancólico: Historias de Nacionalistas Vascos*. Madrid: Espasa Hoy, 1997.

Judt, Tony. *A Grand Illusion? An Essay on Europe*. New York: Hill and Wang, 1996.

Julien, Claude. *Le Canada: Dernière Chance de l'Europe*. Paris: Grasset, 1968.

Kagan, Robert. *Of Paradise and Power: America and Europe in the New World Order.* New York: Alfred A. Knopf, 2003.

Kamen, Henry. *Spain's Road to Empire.* London: Allen Lane, 2002.

Kaplan, William, ed. *Belonging: The Meaning and Future of Canadian Citizenship.* Montreal: McGill-Queen's University Press, 1993.

Kaviraj, Sudipta. "Literature and the Moral Imagination of Modernity." In *The Moral Fabric in Contemporary Societies,* ed. Grazyna Skapska and Annamaria Orla-Bukowska. Leiden: Brill, 2003.

Keating, Michael. *Nations against the State: The New Politics of Nationalism in Quebec, Catalonia and Scotland.* Basingstoke: Macmillan, 1996.

Kleinfeld, Judith and Andrew Kleinfeld. "Cowboy Nation and American Character." *Society* (March-April 2004): 43–50.

Krauss, Clifford. "Canada's View on Social Issues is Opening Rifts with the United States." *New York Times,* 2 December 2003.

Lacombe, Sylvie. *La rencontre de deux peuples élus.* Sainte-Foy: Presses de l'Université Laval, 2002.

Lamonde, Yvan and Claude Corbo, eds. *Le rouge et le bleu: Une anthologie de la pensée politique au Québec de la Conquête à la Révolution tranquille.* Montréal: Presses de l'Université de Montréal, 1999.

Legaré, Anne. *Le Québec otage de ses alliés: Les relations du Québec avec la France et les États-Unis.* Montréal: VLB Éditeur, 2003.

Levitt, Joseph. *Henri Bourassa and the golden calf: the social program of the Nationalists of Quebec (1900–1914).* Ottawa : Les Editions de l'Université d'Ottawa, 1972.

Lipset, Seymour Martin. *Continental Divide, the values and institutions of the United States and Canada.* New York and London: Routledge, 1990.

Maclure, Jocelyn. *Quebec Identity: The Challenge of Pluralism.* Montreal: McGill-Queen's University Press, 2003.

Mair, Charles. *Tecumseh, a drama and Canadian poems.* Toronto: The Radisson Society of Canada, 1926.

Marshall, T.H. *Citizenship and Social Class and Other Essays.* Cambridge: Cambridge University Press, 1950.

MacKinnon, Neil and Alison Luke. "Changes in Identity Attitudes as Reflections of Social and Cultural Change." *Canadian Journal of Sociology* 27, no. 3 (2002): 299–338.

McLachlin, Beverley, Chief Justice of Canada. "The Civilization of Difference." Fourth Annual LaFontaine-Baldwin Lecture, Halifax, 7 March 2003.

McRoberts, Kenneth. *Misconceiving Canada: The Struggle for National Unity.* Toronto: Oxford University Press, 1997.

Meisel, John, Guy Rocher, and Arthur Silver, eds. *As I Recall/ Si je me souviens.* Montreal: Institute for Research on Public Policy, 1999.

Meltzer, Bernard and Gil Richard Musolf. "Resentment and Ressentiment." *Sociological Inquiry* 72, no. 2 (2002): 240–252.

Mill, John Stuart. *Representative Government*. London: Dent, 1968.

David Miller. *On Nationality*. Oxford: Oxford University Press, 1995.

Molina, Antonio Muñoz. "El artista consentido." *El Pais*, 17 April 2004.

Neuhold, Hanspeter. "Transatlantic Turbulence: Rift or Ripples." *European Foreign Affairs Review* 8 (2003): 457-468.

Noel, S.J.R. *Patrons, Clients, Brokers: Ontario Society and Politics, 1791-1896*. Toronto: University of Toronto Press, 1990.

Offe, Claus. "The Democratic Welfare State in an Integrating Europe." In *Democracy Beyond the State?*, ed. Michael Greven and Louis Pauly. Lanham, MD: Rowman and Littlefield, 2000.

Papcke, Sven. "Who Needs European Identity?" In *The Idea of Europe: Problems of National and Transnational Identity*, ed. Brian Nelson, David Roberts, and Walter Veit. New York/Oxford: Berg, 1992.

Pascal, Blaise. *Pensées*. Paris: Le Livre de Poche, 2000.

Patten, Chris. "Who Do They Think We Are? Being British." *The Political Quarterly*, 73, no. 2 (April–June 2002): 125-134.

Pfaff, William. *The Wrath of Nations*. New York: Simon and Schuster, 1993.

Phillips, Kevin. *Boiling Point*. New York: Random House, 1993.

Pinard, Maurice, Robert Bernier, and Vincent Lemieux. *Un combat inachevé*. Sainte-Foy: Les Presses de l'Université du Québec, 1997.

Reikmann, Sonja P. "The Myth of European Unity in Myths and Nationhood." In *Myths and Nationhood*, ed. Geoffrey Hoskins and George Schopflin. London: Hurst, 1997.

Renan, Ernest. *Qu'est ce qu'une nation?* Paris: Agora, 1992.

Rioux, Marcel. *Un peuple dans le siècle*. Montréal: Boréal, 1990.

Robbins, Keith. "The United Kingdom as a Multi-national State." In *Nationalism in Europe: Past and Present*, ed. J. Beramendi, R. Maiz, and X. Nunez. Vol. 2. Santiago de Compostela: Universidad de Santiago de Compostela, 1994.

Rougemont, Denis de. *Vingt-huit siècles d'Europe: la conscience européenne à travers les textes, d'Hésiode à nos jours*. Paris: Payot, 1961.

Roy, Bruno. "Montréal, ville internationale de langue française." *Le Devoir*, 4 May 2004.

Saunders, Doug. "So, our Conservatives aren't progressive any more." *Globe and Mail*, 22 May 2004.

Schmidt, Dennis I. *On Germans and Other Greeks: Tragedy and Ethical Life*. Bloomington: Indiana University Press, 2001.

Schneider, Peter. "Separated by civilization: Trans-Atlantic impasse." *International Herald Tribune*, 7 April 2004. Available online from http://www.iht.com/articles/513613.html.

Schwarzmantel, John. *Citizenship and Identity*. London: Routledge, 2003.

Shore, Cris and Annabel Black. "Citizens' Europe and the Construction of European Identity." In *The Anthropology of Europe*, ed.

Victoria A. Goddard, Joseph Llobera and Cris Shore. Oxford: Berg, 1994.

Siegfried, André. *The Race Question in Canada.* Ed. Frank H. Underhill. 1906. Reprint, Carleton Library Series, no. 29. Ottawa: Carleton University Press, 1966.

Smith, Anthony D. *Nationalism: Theory, Ideology, History.* Cambridge: Polity Press, 2001.

Sutherland, John. "God Save America." *The Guardian,* 4 May 2004.

Thatcher, Margaret. "The European Family of Nations." In *The Eurosceptical Reader,* ed. Martin Holmes. Basingstoke: Palgrave Macmillan, 1996.

Thériault, Joseph Yvon. *Critique de l'américanité: Mémoire et démocratie au Québec.* Montréal: Québec-Amérique, 2002.

Therborn, Göran. "The World's Trader, the World's Lawyer. Europe and Global Resources." *European Journal of Social Theory* 5, no. 4 (November 2002): 403–417.

Tocqueville, Alexis de. *Democracy in America.* Translated by Henry Reeve. Vol. 1. New York: Schocken Books, 1961.

Todorov, Tzvetan. *Nous et les Autres.* Paris: Seuil, 1989.

Trudeau, Pierre-Elliott. "Quebec on the Eve of the Asbestos Strike." In *The Asbestos Strike,* ed. Pierre Trudeau. Toronto: James Lewis & Samuel, 1974.

UNESCO. *World Culture Report 2000.* Paris, 2000.

Venne, Michel, ed. *Vive Quebec!: new thinking and new approaches to the Quebec nation.* Toronto: James Lorimer, 2001.

Vincent, Andrew. *Nationalism and Particularity.* Cambridge: Cambridge University Press, 2002.

Viroli, Maurizio. *For Love of Country: An Essay on Patriotism and Nationalism.* Oxford: Clarendon Press, 1995.

Wallace, William. "Rescue or Retreat? The Nation State in Western Europe, 1945–93." In *The Question of Europe,* ed. Peter Gowan and Perry Anderson. London: Verso, 1997.

Whitman, Walt. *The Complete Poetry and Selected Prose of Walt Whitman,* ed. James E. Miller Jr. Boston: Houghton Mifflin, 1959.

Weiler, J.H.H. "Does Europe Need a Constitution?" In *The Question of Europe,* ed. Peter Gowan and Perry Anderson. London: Verso, 1997.

Weight, Richard. *Patriots: National Identities in Britain, 1940–2000.* Basingstoke: Macmillan, 2002.

Young, Julian. *The Death of God and the Meaning of Life.* London: Routledge, 2003.

Zizek, Slavoj. "What Does Europe Want?" *In These Times,* 1 May 2004.

INDEX